FOR OUR OWN GOOD

Childcare Issues
in Ireland

Bernie Purcell

The Collins Press

Published in 2001 by
The Collins Press
West Link Park
Doughcloyne
Wilton
Cork

British Library Cataloguing in Publication data.

Typesetting by The Collins Press Ltd.

Printed in Ireland by Colour Books Ltd.

ISBN: 1-898256-81-0

CONTENTS

ACKNOWLEDGEMENTS

Many, many people have helped bring this book to fruition, some of whom never knew of its existence, such as Ger who provided stacks of paper before the book had ever been begun! For all of those quirky coincidences of fate and encouragements I thank the universe.

To all the people who assisted me good-naturedly and wholeheartedly, I thank you.

First, I wish to express my deepest gratitude to all of the people, who must remain nameless, who, over the years, have spoken to me formally and informally and provided me with insights into their lives which have contributed to the formulation of my ideas about children and parenting.

To my colleagues at Roebuck Counselling Centre who tirelessly supported this project and inquired about its well-being – thank you, especially Claire, who engaged in constant and frequently lengthy conversations about childcare. To all of you, thanks. I couldn't have done it without you or the house.

To my good friends Ann and Dolores who helped edge things along whenever I met or spoke with them. Thank you for those intimate chats and your belief in the value of such a book.

My own family of origin, their extended families and my partner's family, all provided me with the impetus to keep going.

Thank you to all the organisations who provided me with the information, in particular Barnardos, National Women's Council of Ireland, Department of Education, Department of Health and Children, Eastern Regional Health Authority, Central Statistics Office, Economic and Social Research Institute, National Childminders Association, the Adoption

Board, Parentline, Parental Equality Support Group, Employment Equality Agency, Foroige, Dyslexia Association of Ireland and the Swedish Embassy.

To Freda who is a true mentor, gentle inspiring and ever soul-searching. To Margaret for her patience and endurance, her endless typing and good humour amidst what looked at times like raw chaos. To Billy for searching out those vital bits of information. A heartfelt thanks to all.

Finally, and most especially, thanks to my partner Jack, who has been my partner for almost half the years I've been on this planet and my enthusiastic, wildly energetic children. Thank you Jack for your special brand of non-intrusive love and care.

BERNIE PURCELL
JANUARY 2001

PERSONAL PREFACE

It's a funny thing about life; if you refuse to accept anything but the best, you very often get it.

Somerset Maugham

I was born in the mid-1950s in rural Ireland and grew up in an era of mass emigration when Ireland offered little to those seeking opportunity or adventure. The Catholic Church reigned omnipotently in a sectarian society. In the community where I lived, private and public life merged, with people having little individual privacy. It was an insular, suffocating beginning; strict codes of behaviour and attitude prevailed. People displayed an amazing capacity to have prolonged conversations about nothing, especially not themselves; the 'say nothing' mentality which John McGahern describes so well in his books about that period. My initial years of schooling were spent in a cold barrack-like primary school where corporal punishment was meted out daily. Yet those years were wild, free and exciting compared to the cerebral, restrictive years of my convent secondary school. However, I encountered some inspiring teachers who passionately loved their subject and teaching. It became clear to me that education was the way forward, or indeed the way out of, a humdrum existence.

I went to University College Dublin in the 1970s and it was as if all my dreams had come true. The world I entered was an exploding cosmos of opportunity, explorative and challenging; I was awed by the amount of stimulation. Summers spent travelling were just as vital a part of those years as college education; it seemed such a pity to spend summers in Ireland when the world beckoned! Tasting something of other cultures only whetted my appetite for more. College led on to the world of work and marriage, both of which I entered into in the late 1970s.

The conception of my first child in 1984, a much desired and longed for circumstance, coincided with an opportunity for a career change; an opportunity for which I was undeniably grateful but which entailed longer working hours, less holidays and less pay. By the time of his birth, I was still relatively new to my changed career and had taken on further training in psychotherapy; so I took little maternity leave.

As an adult, I had always felt that I determined my own life. I had been married for six years before deciding to become pregnant and only did so after many hours of discussions and reflection with my partner and friends. Unlike my mother, who had had eight children, I didn't in any way feel that marriage was about having children or that giving birth had to be an integral part of the female experience, so I was very consciously choosing parenthood. Nevertheless, everything was changed for me by that experience. It was as if I were seeing the world for the first time; the suffering, the vulnerability and wonderment of people touched me in a new, more immediate manner. I felt as if I'd woken up. The expansion of consciousness was similar to what I experienced, many years later, at my mother's death. For the first time in my life, I knew and understood how someone could choose to give their life for someone else. If necessary, I knew I'd die for this little being, so vulnerable and so dependent on me. It was nothing to do with heroics, it was simply how things were. As one friend put it to me, 'After I had a baby, I saw every child differently; every child was my baby, my baby was every child, every child suffering, starving, not being cared for'. I knew and understood all of my mother's worries and anguish about us as children, her fears and concerns about how the world would treat us. Nothing could have prepared me for the overwhelming love I experienced for this little wailing bundle, abruptly ensconced in my life, who seemed adorable even at 3am!

As a mother working outside the home, I was now entering the arena of dualisms. I wanted to be as good as I possibly could at my job and perform at my peak, despite being awake at night or a child being sick at home. At the same time, I wanted to be an excellent mother and be joyous, playful, patient and fun-loving, despite being exhausted from work. For me, at that time, both of these realities existed quite separately and it seemed important to hide any difficulties I was experiencing lest my job motivation and skill be questioned. Though grieving the separation from my child, I believed that I should either stay home full-time, which I didn't want to do, or opt to work outside the home; and if I chose that, then there was no point in moaning about it. I considered my conflictual feelings my own personal problem and not part of the universal dilemma for working mothers. Older women, who had already traversed this emotional quagmire and found their solution in staying home full-time when children were little and returning to work later, offered little consolation. Peers who decided to stay home full-time to care for their children sighed in relief, assured of their decision in the face of such conflictual emotion. The only advice the veterans had, the women who had gone out to work in the preceding harsher years, was if you wanted to work then you must harden your heart against your own and your baby's needs.

Now fifteen years, three more children and many career changes later, I can say that my home life and professional work are no longer in conflict. For about six or seven years now I've experienced this flow and harmony. My days are busy, but not manic. I serve my children's needs and my own heart by organising my work schedule to fit their lives, not vice versa. I take the same holidays as my children, working a little if it slots in with other activities and plans, but I now never work away from home. My children don't pay a price because I have a career and we have financial ease. One of my most difficult memories from my children's childhoods is an occasion when I returned from a week-long work trip abroad to find that my son, less than a year old, didn't recognise me. Imagine how that was for him. It has taken a lot of changes, assessments, listening to my children and a supportive and loving partner, who also wanted to ensure a lot of time and connection with the children, to bring it about.

Along the way, there were many conflicts and difficulties, but always it was possible to find solutions once we remained open. My husband went to college, did further training and changed his career. During that time I was the sole earner. We moved to the country at one stage, thinking it would be a better environment for the children to grow up in, but after a short while had to admit defeat because of the travelling and moved back to the city, retaining the house as a holiday home. I did further study, which again meant doing course work late at night or early in the morning. To date, I am now in my fourth career and my partner is easing towards his third. I have been a teacher, a psychotherapist, director of a counselling/psychotherapy centre and now a writer.

Two constants remained in my children's lives, both of which offered them a security; they've had the same childminders (relatives) and they remained in the same school. When they were young and said they wanted to have me at home more, I knew for their happiness and mine I had to find solutions and do just that. I've listened to the inklings of doubt in myself and those of my children, not knowing how I would resolve something. But always, once I was willing to understand that change was required, then solutions emerged. With the birth of my fourth child came the decision to have him cared for only by myself or my partner up to the age of two to three years.

Most of my problems were solved by becoming self-employed. Now I only had to be concerned with the work I wanted to do, earning a living and getting adequate time with my children: other people's requirements were taken out of the equation. Decisions like having work brought to me instead of travelling to different work venues proved invaluable. This was facilitated by buying a very large house to run my business from and live in: precious hours spent commuting were erased, and any work breaks could be spent with my children. In time, my need for work colleagues necessitated additional innovations: we converted the large house into our work-place and built a house to live in at the bottom of the garden!

I'm not suggesting that becoming self-employed is the answer for everyone. There is no holiday or sick pay and no maternity leave; all of these responsibilities are yours, requiring that you plan ahead. Choosing as a parent to be employed or self-employed merely gives you a different set of quandaries. But it may well be necessary to be open to changes not already considered that will improve the whole family's quality of life. It's important just to ask yourself: are you doing it all the way you'd really want and if not, what would you want to change? Some changes can be implemented very fast but some need a lot of planning and may take up to two years to fully bring about. Equally I'm aware that parenting is a shifting and volatile conundrum of emotions and events. A decision made one year may not be workable the following year, so one is always assessing and adapting. There is not going to be just one decision which will solve matters. There may be one decision for now, followed by numerous others along the way – it's about a style of living, it's about process.

It is ludicrous, though, how little time we spend preparing for the conflicts and difficulties which parenting brings. Couples may spend up to a year planning, organising and preparing for a wedding yet not think beyond the actual birth of their newborn. This can bring about a cycle of reaction, with overworked and exhausted parents merely surviving. Add another child or two to this scenario and it becomes really difficult for employed parents to even get time to think about possibilities or solutions, apart from the obvious one of one parent remaining at home and being the main carer.

This book offers the opportunity to assess the childcare situation here in Ireland and ask 'Are we doing well enough?' It aims to combine the personal and political questions pertaining to childcare. It is not sufficient to point the finger at state policies and demand change: it is imperative that individual childcare arrangements be considered. Neither is it feasible to consider that one parent or two can take on the entire responsibility for getting things right in a state where neither adequate support nor assistance for family needs exist. Employers must be required to involve themselves in seeking resolutions which benefit their employees who are parents. Childcare and parenting must be endorsed within the sphere of the working lives of parents in a way we have not yet seen.

Certainly we are providing more materially for our children than any previous generation, and in a society where our ancestors were starving only 150 years ago, that may give us a lot of reassurance. Children are more articulate, better able to name their needs and desires, better listened to and less beaten (though not less sexually abused, unfortunately). But bearing in mind all that we now know about children's needs for contact with parents, stability and nurturance, are they better cared for?

I've wished to write this book for a long time for both professional and personal reasons. As a mother who has had a career for all my children's lives, I understand intimately the dilemmas which arise. As a psychotherapist I've borne witness to, over and over again, the problems incurred by adults who have experienced deficient parenting. I've also encountered many whose lives were relatively comfortable and who had experienced many privileges in life and still parented inadequately. I've sat with the children of both these groupings and helped them in their struggle to be heard. As a teacher I've experienced how the educational system fails, not just the students, but also the teachers.

I've been a teacher for six years, a psychotherapist specialising in treating adults and teenagers who've been the victims of sexual or physical violence in either childhood or adulthood, for seven years, I've worked in private practice dealing with a wide range of problems for five years. I've been Director of the

Dublin Rape Crises Centre and Roebuck Counselling Centre for a combination of ten years. I've trained and supervised others working in the caring professions and thereby had access to thousands of cases. Over time I've come to understand that those workers were not doing so well in their own childminding choices. No parent is exempt from the issues discussed in this book.

As human beings responsible for the world we are creating, we need to ask more of ourselves then the gratification of our personal needs. If we, as a society and as individuals, can commit to prioritising parenting we will be richly rewarded.

Chapter 1

CHILDHOOD

As Irish citizens entering the twenty-first century, we are original. Over recent decades parenting, families, patterns of marriage, child care, child rearing and our economic situation have changed utterly. Returning awe-struck emigrants can hardly recognise the country they left ten or twenty years ago. While most of these innovations have brought a coveted freedom and a richness of choice heretofore excluded from Irish culture, there is a price, at least one gaping area where all is not well. As men and women thrust forward to new territories, zoom in on the shackles and restrictions separately binding them and independently pursue their dreams and possibilities, what is happening to our children? To whose care are they being entrusted? How well in this thriving, forward-looking country are we taking care of our most cherished beings, our children?

We continue to be made aware of the awful suffering experienced by children in the past in terms of physical and sexual abuse; this may serve to confirm for us that the life of the child in Ireland has greatly improved. Equally we continue to be made aware of poverty, homelessness and addiction issues related to children. The plight of young, single mothers coping with deprivation and isolation is brought to the fore. Crimes committed by children lacking parental supervision are highlighted in the news. These issues are relevant to the Ireland we find ourselves in today. However, this is not the focus of this book. Such problems are stark and horrible and everyone will agree that our society is failing such children. In this book, such problems will indeed be referenced and of course they must be addressed, but the main focal point of the book is children, not obviously deprived (and certainly not materially homeless or drug-addicted), but average children, engaged in life and modern living. As Isaiah Berlin says in *The Crooked Timber of Humanity* , 'The children have obtained what their parents and grandparents longed for – greater freedom, greater material welfare, a juster society; but the old ills are forgotten, and the children face new problems brought about by the very solutions of the old ones'. My contention is that children today, ordinary children, average children, whom nobody will see as having problems, are being asked to manage and negotiate things in their lives previously unrequested of Irish children. Difficulties and dilemmas are being set in motion, things which we probably hardly perceive as difficulties.

Isn't this what happened in the past? Things occurred and continued to occur because they were the norm. Once something was happening all around, people reassured themselves that it must be okay or that there was some reason for it, despite inner inklings of unease or pangs of conscience. But the children knew it was wrong. I, as a child in an average primary school, knew it was wrong that the same children were victimised and beaten, day after day. The children selected for such victimisation were already the least protected in that society. The difference now is that we could choose to see these current problems now, not in ten or twenty years' time, we could choose to inform ourselves now, and we could choose to rectify things. We know children are affected by what happens to them, by the care they do or do not receive and the world they live in, and we could use that consciousness to determine our behaviour in relation to them. This generation cannot plead ignorance. Information abounds about children, childcare and children's rights and needs. We can choose to inform ourselves, to know and understand the lot of the child today. Next time, there will be no major perpetrators of evil such as institutions or systems, to carry the blame, it will be all of us who are blameworthy. It will be us, the ordinary parents, perceiving ourselves to be doing our best and thereby no great wrong, and it will be the state.

In a thriving economy where the term 'Celtic Tiger' trips off everyone's tongue, it may be hard to believe that all matters are not so optimistic. Trapped in the belief that our newfound financial expansion has brought improvements to all levels of our existence, we career on into greater and greater chaos regarding our children and childcare. Look at our childcare system – the worst in the EU. Look at our maternity leave and system for early childhood care. Yet we continue to encourage women to work outside the home. This is appropriate, but without the necessary childcare programmes in place, children will suffer. Ireland is unique in the high number of children we have and the rapidly increasing rate of young mothers working outside the home. Yet the childcare system is not there to support this.

Parents today struggle to give the best to their children. Parents and children are involved in heavy schedules to provide this 'best'; weekends and evenings are taken up by exhausted parents chauffeuring children to extra-curricular activities in the endeavour to provide all of the stimuli deemed necessary. We have special classes for children with a high IQ; nobody is to be apathetic or unstimulated. The best pedagogy for everything is ferreted out, from music teaching to tennis coaching. Talents are spotted where there is barely an embryonic interest. Boredom has become a deplorable emotion, to be eradicated. Exciting amusement and entertainment are the order of the day: everything must be maintained at an interesting level of stimulation. When children are not taking part in organised activities, they are spending long hours watching television or playing computer games. Children are receiving less physical exercise than previous generations and obesity in children is becoming more common. The first 'fat camp' recently opened in Britain. In a society which overstimulates, we may forget the positive creativity that can emerge from boredom, the wonderful play, alone or with others, which can be richly woven from an imagination allowed to roam.

Each summer I see my own children, city children with structured lives, relax into an extended period in our summer-house by the beach. Nothing is organised, computers and play stations remain in the city, and they merge into a time of dream-like ease with other holidaying city kids. Endless play and games are created and recreated the following day, with the inclusion of parents at some events or on some occasions for supervisory purposes. Each year I give thanks that they are fortunate enough to have this experience. Working parents are not usually able to schedule their holidays to extend to those of the school holidays and lots of children, therefore, continue their winter routines into summer, attending summer camps and activities, and experience little free, unplanned time anywhere in their calendar. Easter and even Christmas vacations now present the option of activity camps.

Are we over-involved? asks Diana Ehrensaft in *Spoiling Childhood*. She speaks of well-meaning but confused American parents spinning from over-indulgence and over-involvement to abandonment of their offspring. We fail to provide what is required and necessary to their healthy psychological growth, and then appease with over-indulgence in a manner which offers little. This discrepancy leads to insecurity and uncertainty for the child. In a chapter entitled 'Parenting by guilt', Ehrensaft talks of 'middle-class parents who have gone after what they wanted – career, money, happiness – sometimes at the expense of their children's well-being and yet who also act as if the sky is the limit for their children. These parents indulge their sons and daughters and cater to their children's every whim, they do their children's homework with or for them, they let their children throw terrible epithets at them. Then they turn around and leave their children for long periods of time, too long, while they complete a work project or follow their own muse.' There is little time for, or emphasis on, easy-going, non-focused, laid back family time where children and parents simply relax together. Such non-focused time provides the backbone of sustainable relationships. If a family always has to be actively involved in some pursuit together, it may seem that the activity is more important than the togetherness.

Penelope Leach equally names abandonment as part of the modern malaise and is sharply critical of our current child-minding arrangements. 'Naturally parents who are seeking more and more day care for younger and younger infants are looking for economic improvement in their own lives, but not many would do so if they believed that they earned money at their children's expense.' If we say that long hours spent with childminders are not good for children, the way that men and women hear that can be quite different. Women understand they're being told they oughtn't to work outside the home. Men often agree with the statement but don't see that they have to be part of the solution. I'm still amazed how young men becoming fathers can believe that it is not going to infringe on their working life while women, during the pregnancy, will be busily anticipating the forthcoming changes.

I don't believe in an either-or situation, the sacrificial model, as I call it, the syndrome of the 1950s and 1960s where many women stayed home full-time to care for their children, mostly out of duty and a sense of obligation. Mothers staying at home full-time to care for their children is no guarantee of good parenting. We are in the era of choice and responsibility and must use both wisely. Much more is being asked of parents today; they must be responsible to themselves, to each other and for their children. Everyone knows that unhappy people make unhappy parents and that children can be affected negatively by parents not pursuing their own dreams. As Carl Jung said, 'nothing has a more powerful influence upon children than the life their parents have not lived'. But balance must be brought to bear in every situation. Children need their parents; traditionally they have had very little access to their fathers but if now they have less and less access to their mothers this is not progress. In every scenario, we have the possibility, individually and collectively as a society, of progressing or regressing. We need to be alert to our decisions and question our choices. We are on such a threshold now. Things are changing very fast – the decisions we make now regarding our children, family and working lives will take a long time to undo if they are defective. We need to be wise. Progress is not simply a linear movement; we are at risk of progressing economically and materially but incurring huge deficits in the area of human responsibilities.

In this era the personal and the political are merging. The 1990s have seen almost every institution which people trusted and believed in in Ireland exposed for foul and unfair dealings. The trend continues. Hypocrisy of every kind has been brought to public notice. And when the people of Ireland believed they knew all, there was still more. Outside of Ireland similar trends were occurring: dictators were brought to task and presidents were challenged. We have become more and more educated about what leadership is not, by witnessing so much corruption and so many exposures. We are less sure about what it is. People talk of building character and principles and these are perhaps hallmarks of leadership abilities. Certainly the era of the charismatic, sharp-witted, smart mover is nearing its close. People are being held responsible for their actions. As everyone knows, those people who avidly seek power may not prove to be the best leaders, or the most insightful, but they will work to get it. The person who obtains and maintains power through coercion, manipulation and fear will find it harder to locate a place for such traits in the future in Ireland. A realism has been brought about, but it is an optimistic realism which seeks decency, authenticity and competency.

Parents are leaders, seeking to instil values and abilities in their children which will help them to fulfil their dreams and ultimately live worthwhile lives. Children, however, often are exposed to the best and the worst of their parents because parenting takes place within the realms of human dynamics. Parents need support to parent well, to understand their responsibilities to their children, and to ensure their children bring forth their best talents in a variety of settings. Those who fail to fulfil their duties will, perhaps more than any previous generation, receive criticism from children who are being brought up to be perceptive, challenging and articulate. Will we be able to answer to our children? Will we be capable of explaining why, in an economically thriving time, we are not choosing to prioritise the care of our children in so many obvious ways, and thereby not equipping them for their futures?

Our children, as adults, are going to be required to manage family life, intimacy, relationships, and the challenges of a changing work environment without the old guidelines. As restrictions continue to be removed, then more is required of the individual. An ability to be part of an interdependent structure is necessary, otherwise things will continue to disintegrate without the necessary rebuilding occurring. Parents have a great deal to oversee and be responsible for in bringing up children, but that ought not to be without the support of the state.

Like parents, teachers are leaders, *in loco parentis*, and can exert positive influences on children and teenagers. Day-schools, particularly secondary schools, which ought to involve wholesome preparation for the adult years, still maintain a strong academic slant. Teaching methods do little to teach an ability to communicate or anything about discourse. Regurgitation is still the main skill learned, with the exception of subjects like art and woodwork which offer an opportunity to make decisions and create. Teachers are frequently defensive and unskilled in interpersonal dialogue, yet will be employed on the basis of their academic ability. They begin teaching, receive very little support or encouragement, meet very meagre opportunities to challenge their thinking, assess their teaching methods or create new possibilities, and merely flounder in a system which has already served them badly as students. They do not work from the most talented aspects of themselves because no process exists whereby they are encouraged to find and work from that germ of excellence. They struggle under terrible pressure and merely pass that on. Teachers can succeed in making any subject boring or interesting depending on their ability to respect, communicate and be open to the pupils.

Why aren't students asked for feedback? I've spoken to hundreds of young people who admirably articulate what works with them and what doesn't. Who asks them? Students can clearly identify what they term constitutes a 'good teacher': someone who enjoys their work, is passionate about life and shows the students respect. Possibilities of linking pay increases to performance in the classroom have, understandably, incurred strong opposition from teacher's unions. But bringing about greater accountability is necessary, and while that won't be achieved by looking at exam results, there are other measures. Principals must be allowed to exert, and indeed be answerable themselves to the Department for exerting, some kinds of assessment procedures. The best types of assessment procedures actively involve those being assessed in that process. Teachers must be required to become accountable in terms of teaching methods, knowledge of their subject and ability to relate to students.

The teaching of life-skills or interpersonal skills frequently occurs in individual classes or in Transition Year. Such skills must form an integral part of the teacher-pupil communication and the subjects. Development of personality cannot be crammed into Transition Year before students return to the 'real' work of school for the next two years – two years where the only assessment of the person will be academic. The narrowness of what they learn is breathtaking. They spend six months of each year in school from 9am - 4pm approximately for five or six years of secondary school; could we not do more?

The emphasis, as always, is on the children who are not academically able. Different options and choices are offered, but not enough. Children need to have experiences of competence and success in order to build confidence. But, what about the children who succeed well academically? Everyone agrees that we are failing the children who do badly or opt out of school but we are also failing, dreadfully, the children who succeed. In a system of success and failure, one is never far away from the fear of failure however well one is doing. What are children learning about success? What are they learning about themselves that will have an enduring, enhancing impact on their future lives? Very little, I think. They are learning plenty which will help them to be dysfunctional in their lives, unfortunately. Stephen Covey has begun to challenge the idea that one can be a true leader in any sphere if one doesn't know how to live and prioritise one's life in terms of understanding your responsibility to those around you. Are we teaching our children to recognise themselves as both independent and interdependent beings, responsible not just for themselves but for how they treat others? Are we teaching them that to be happy and fulfilled they will need to be moral beings, refraining from acts of destruction towards themselves, others, other creatures or the planet, and that monetary opulence can bring only limited happiness and satisfaction? If we were providing these opportunities in the teenage years we would succeed in sending young adults into the world equipped for their future.

Of course, parents have the right to educate their children at home and a percentage do so. The newly-formed 'Home Education Network' (HEN) has 100 members and approximately 200 families are currently educating their children at home. While this continues to remain an option, perhaps a necessity, for some parents, school could offer a great deal more in terms of social development and peer learning than it currently does.

A further problem, identified by Ehrensaft, is the 'overvaluing' of our children. Given the Irish psyche of low self-esteem, we may feel there could be no such thing. As a culture we are emerging collectively from a time of oppression, struggle and sparse opportunity. On the world stage it's a good time to be Irish but we need to maintain a sense of realism and steadiness. Ehrensaft is in fact outlining a very real predicament which occurs when the child becomes a product of the parents' own narcissism. The child is absorbed into the parents' lives and expectations; now is the chance to get it right and perfection is sought. The child is put under 'unseen' pressure to be significant and do well. To anyone observing, it probably looks fine that the parents think so well of the child and want so much for him. But notice the parental anxiety; too much is at stake here, the child's interest and motivation are being compromised. My eldest son, when he was little, responded rather humorously one day to my husband's ardent interest in his learning the violin with, 'Sounds like you'd enjoy it, dad, maybe you should take it up!' A separate and autonomous space must be created for the child. As Kahlil Gibran so eloquently puts it;

> *Your children are not your children.*
> *They are the sons and daughters of life's longing for itself.*
> *They come through you but not from you, and though they are*
> *with you yet they belong not to you.*

Predictability as a stable, sustaining force in a child's life is waning. Life partners, homes, minders and schools change frequently and children are expected to adapt and be successful, pleasing, articulate and independent. They are expected to absorb major life changes without great difficulty and move on. They, unfairly, are relied upon to form relationships easily and suspend them equally easily while still remaining open and communicative. Children are naturally trusting and mostly want to please the adults in their lives and make the best of situations. They will endeavour to adapt, but if too much is asked of them and too many changes are thrust upon them, they will begin to react. They will seek to protect themselves psychologically by withdrawing from that trust and openness. Adults need to be responsible in the amount of changes they ask their children to shoulder. Being able to anticipate the players in your world has a calming, restorative influence. Children love doing the same things, with the same people, in the same way, either at/for specific occasions or in a regular ongoing fashion. It is not possible for them to constantly experience major changes in their world without being hurt and damaged.

Everybody wants to be happy; second, third and fourth

long-term adult relationships are entered into with alarming swiftness. While this may have detrimental consequences for the adults, it most certainly will predispose the children involved to insecurity and distrust about adult relationships: happiness is constantly pursued outside of the self, others embody our happiness and joy and then we blame them as soon as they fall from grace. This is the era of feelings and emotions; what we feel is elevated to a higher plane. If we feel we love someone then we do, however short term. Long-term partners to whom solid vows and commitments were made are discarded easily and without guilt. Children are being asked to bear witness to such losses and disappointments over and over again, as well as dealing with their parents' sexuality. Sometimes it seems that all the energy and time in a family goes towards dealing with the parental dilemmas instead of giving children a solid arena from which to face their choices and decisions. Stephen Covey suggests that it's time to revert to love as an action verb, something we do, something we actively engage in, not something we are powerless about. 'If our feelings control our actions, it is because we have abdicated our responsibility and empowered them to do so.'

It is imperative that children have an experience of parents who are able to take charge of their lives instead of chasing dreams which crumble in the face of reality. Facing oneself is a difficult matter and can be facilitated by a long-term relationship which is supportive, yet challenging. But it is not something which is sweet and endearing; you may be faced with a very nasty side of yourself and your partner, and it requires enormous courage to continue to commit to a relationship. 'Conflict itself is of course a sign of health,' as Maslow said.

Seeing couples separating, I'm frequently appalled by how quickly things become so nasty. Values like decency and fairness wane and war is declared, a war of 'intimate enemies' as Goleman names it. It seems that when people no longer accommodate or suit each other they are no longer 'in love' and can be dispensed with. I suggest such people never loved each other in anything but a superficial narcissistic way which pertained to the self but not beyond. The problem is that the children of this marriage are in the war zone and there is nowhere for them to take cover. They do not deserve such disregard. Parents need to be able to extricate themselves from a relationship they no longer wish to be in without involving the children. This may mean that the actual leaving needs to be slowed down and the separating partners move towards the final separation over months. Mostly what happens is that couples separate without really dealing with the many difficult stages of that process and then spill out their grief, anger and disappointment all over the children. The jaggedness of most separations means that children spend years dealing with aspects of the separation which aren't really their business; their own loss will be great and that should be what they are encouraged to focus on.

With all the changes in relationships that children now encounter, they are merely becoming more skilled at managing and more expert at adapting. This mind-set will not form the foundation or substance for healthy living. Such underpinnings will create will-o-the-wisps who can adapt to anything and who will expect little in terms of intimacy in their adult lives.

One of my sons recently began secondary school and has been encountering a lot of difficulty in the transition. After many discussions he was finally able to name the problem for himself. He was missing the strength of relationship that he'd experienced all through primary school. For six years he'd had three female teachers (each for two years) who built strong relationships with him, and he felt affirmed and cared for by each of these women in turn. Now his experience was that he didn't matter – his form teacher only met him once or twice a week and that was obviously too little to sustain him. As he continued to try and manage over the months and I attempted to assist him in his difficulty, I reflected on how difficult it must be for many children who have to negotiate changes in terms of who they live with. My son's home life was relatively stable, he had remained in the same school and had maintained his core friendships and still things were difficult for him. As parents, we are blind to the difficulties of our children; we simply choose not to see, thereby leaving them to cope with and face circumstances that they are not in the least equipped to face. Relationships are the cornerstone of a child's life. Depending on the strength or weakness of their primary relationships, they can be led towards trust and affection or desolation.

Frequently childcare concerns simplistically run aground on the issue of whether or not women should work outside the home. People take up strong positions for and against and feel that holding the argument in this terrain will create some clarity. But this is only one strand in a whole series of concerns which we need to take into account when speaking about the issue of how we are caring for our children. Therefore this is not a book about whether or not women should work outside the home, defined by Jayne Buxton as 'The Mother War', the Superwoman versus the Earthmother. Like Buxton, I make the presumption that this is not a useful conflict to enter – the tyranny of both of these positions has shadowed women for too long. It is time to entrust to the ordinary working woman a place of respect in our society – it is not a time for heroines. Surely it is possible for people to pursue fulfilling careers in fewer than 40/50 hours a week. I believe women, like men, must include it as their right to continue to make a contribution in the workplace while at the same time becoming parents: the solution doesn't lie in women giving up that right. That would be a retrogressive step.

In a piece of research by Broom which compared parental responsiveness to children in dual-earner and single-earner families, it was found that 'marital quality and psychological well-being are important supports of sensitive parenting for dual-earner and single-earner families alike'. In other words healthy people make wise choices about their adult relationships and create healthy environments for their children to grow up in. As everyone knows, parents can spend a lot of time with children and do a really bad job; simply being with your children is no guarantee of good parenting. In a report commissioned by eight Irish health boards and published in December 1999, 'Best Health For Children', the development of a national parent support strategy was recommended.

This generation of parents may have had to cope as children with physical chastisement, fear of adults, repressed sexuality and sparse displays of physical affection. Generally speaking, these issues are not major factors in children's experiences today. The problems are nevertheless complex and will have devastating effects if not dealt with adequately.

I'm espousing the idea of formulating a structure outside of corporate and economic values where no one loses, where no one has to pay the price. Utopia, the cynics might shrug, but it is possible now to change matters. It may be harder in a few more years as our style of living spins more and more out of our control. I'm speaking of developing a situation where, within the family dynamic, the father isn't burdened with the sole financial responsibility, isn't forced to work all his days or all his hours to stay ahead. Statistics Canada recently published data which showed that health risks are greater for those working more than 40 hours a week. People tend to put on weight and increase tobacco and alcohol intake. Those who moved from a normal working week, 35-40 hours to 41 or over, were deemed to have increased the risk of damage to their health. I'm envisaging a setting where the mother working outside the home doesn't have to do two jobs or be guilt-ridden about her choices, and where children have the experience of being parented by both parents, getting ample time with both, and are also spared the experience of spending long hours with minders or being cared for by stressed-out overworked parents. Our values must be refocused solidly in the realm of interpersonal relationships and we must attend successfully to those in our care.

In order to do that a number of things must happen. Citizens must be educated to consider the responsibility of parenthood as the lofty task it is, prior to actually becoming parents. Young people and couples need to be taught the significance of the role they take on in becoming parents. Children need to have the experience of being well parented by parents who are capable of working together and adapting circumstances and situations to encompass the needs of all the members of that unit.

This book asks you, the reader, to assess your own situation and be open to questions. Are you squandering the relationships with your children and if so what can you do to rectify matters? It is not simply a question of complaining about what our government is not doing (and there is plenty to complain about), it is also about deciding what you, or you and your partner, can do to address matters and then doing it. I know many, many people who have changed their lives and styles of living in order to encompass elements they felt were necessary for the enhancement of their family lives. If you feel the way you are living is not okay for the people you are responsible for, don't panic. Firstly begin to focus on what is not okay and then actively set about finding solutions. Seek help and advice, be tenacious. Don't despair. Persevere and solutions will be found.

This is a book encouraging you to look at your value system and that of our society. Are you out of kilter with what's important to you? Just consider the following points:

- What is important to you?
- Does your life reflect this?
- Is your work enhancing to you and does it reflect your values?
- Do you make sufficient income for your own needs and that of your family? (In considering monetary needs keep in mind the advice of Benjamin Franklin 'A wise man will desire no more that what he may get justly, use soberly, distribute cheerfully, and leave contentedly.')
- What would your partner say about your life?
- What would your children say about you?
- What would members of your family of origin say?
- What would your work colleagues have to say?
- Are you capable of including all those viewpoints in

considering your life?
- Is your life balanced, taking account of all aspects that you must be responsible for?
- What would you like your life to say?

If you are a parent, you may not agree with and/or be irritated by some of the subject matter in this book. Just try to be as honest with yourself as you possibly can be, knowing that in the end it is your life, your responsibilities, your choices. No one else except yourself may ever notice the difference! But those you are responsible for will feel the impact, whether they are aware of it or not.

Chapter 2

THE FABRIC OF IRISH LIFE

Some of the factors contributing to the changes we're experiencing have become synonymous with Irish life, e.g. the comparatively large size of our families, while others have come into existence relatively recently. All of these components are relevant and form part of the modern jigsaw which defines the contextual fabric for our children, child-rearing and childminding. The most important of these components are: the changing roles of women and men; the growth of the economy; the rights of children; changes in parenting and in families; marital breakdown and lone parenting; developments in the workplace; the role of the Catholic church; and changing life expectancy.

WOMEN

The position and role of women have changed significantly over the last twenty years, from the traditional models which we held onto longer than our European neighbours. Today's mothers are likely to be better educated, more economically secure, enjoy greater financial competency, hold more responsible work positions, and be more assertive about their personal needs than their predecessors. More women are working outside the home than ever before; 42 per cent of mothers with children under fifteen years of age are in employment as compared with only 24 per cent of mothers of children older than fifteen years. For the first time in Great Britain more women than men are going out to work, including 65 per cent of married or

17

cohabiting mothers and 40 per cent of lone mothers. The 1997 European Force Survey indicated that the rate was 48.1 per cent for married women, with Sweden experiencing the highest rate at 65.7 per cent. The participation rate among younger Irish mothers with children under five is nearly up to the European average, but it is still low for older women who are married and do not have children or with older children over fifteen.

Women's educational standards have risen, with many full-time mothers availing of the opportunity to participate in retraining or third level education when their children are older. According to the Medium Term Report on the Irish Economy published by the Economic and Social Research Institute (ESRI) the biggest change in women working has occurred among women with higher education in their forties. 'Between 1988 and 1994 the participation rate for this group rose by around twenty percentage points indicating that a significant number of such women, who had been out of the labour force in 1988, had returned to it by 1994.' All of this confirms what we already know: the current need for childcare facilities and services is unprecedented.

The Equality Authority reports show that people defined as engaged in home duties, i.e. not working outside the home, are predominantly women; in 1993 the female share was 98.5 per cent. Surveys still indicate, though, that women spend more time on housework than men and where women are working full-time, they spend three times the amount of time men do on household chores, indicating that women who work full-time may be trying to do two jobs instead of one and a half (the other half being covered by their partner). Shirley Conran, author of the 1975 best-seller *Superwoman*, on her return to Britain after living abroad for twenty years, said recently, 'The change in British woman seems astonishing. They are highly successful in the workplace but they lead their lives in a frenzy of doing'. The same is true for Irish women; they are taking up positions in the workplace but are paying too high a price for that right.

MEN

The role of men is equally in transition; expectations are changing about what it is to be a good father. Increasingly fathers are expected to be emotionally involved in their children's lives, capable of responding to a wide variety of circumstances and needs. Fathers are now expected to be 'emotionally literate'. Fast receding is the sole earner father whose professional life and contribution to society is solidly bolstered by his wife's supportive love and care and raising of the children. Parents now often have quite different careers, work very different schedules, travel and perhaps work in different cities and counties. Fathers are the exclusive breadwinners in only half of all families in Ireland.

The male 'provider role' of the traditional marriage has been under challenge for the past 30 years but Irish society still hasn't made the complete transition. The idea of equal financial responsibility is still daunting for Irish women. They like to keep open the possibility of withdrawal from the workforce if it becomes too intimidating. Women must see it as their responsibility to financially support their families alongside their partners if the provider role is to be laid to rest. And laid to rest it must be if we are to acknowledge and respond to everyone's needs in a family. The provider role, according to Pepper Schwartz in *Peer Marriage: how love between equals really works*, orients the non-provider to the other's needs and the children's needs, rather than the husband and wife to each other and mutually to the family. Of course, as long as men make a better living it remains difficult for women to move forward.

Despite the Organisation of Working Time Act 1997 which put the maximum working week at 48 hours, fathers still work an average of 46 hours per week while one-third work 50 hours or more. This is higher than most of our EU counterparts, e.g. Denmark's average is 41 hours. Conversely, mothers who work outside the home work an average of 31-32 hours per week. Men's work continues to be a crucially defining part of their lives, but the demands from both children and partner for a connected relationship bring a restraint to this aspiration. Building and maintaining relationships with the family requires energy and effort, and home is no longer a place of repose and reprieve after a hard day's work. The man returns home now to a series of other demands and requests which necessitate 'work' of a different nature.

According to Burgess in *Fatherhood Reclaimed: The Making of the Modern Father*, good fathering and mothering are not so different. 'The message emanating from this is that there is no free ride for fatherhood, no magical role for fathers just because they are fathers or just because they are men. It is what each man gives on a personal level that makes him a key player in his child's development.' Tension and conflict may be created by these demands, because anything that beckons men away from the public world of work can constitute a threat to their identity according to Lynn Segal in *Slow Motion: Changing masculinities, Changing men*. Add to this the syndrome identified by Deborah Tannen in her book, *You Just Don't Understand*, when she speaks of the differences in men and women's style of verbal communication, how misunderstood that communication can be and how much each needs to understand and struggle in order to dialogue completely.

Working as a psychotherapist, I encountered many men who were deeply unhappy in their jobs and would have welcomed an opportunity for retraining or time out of the 'provider' position. Yet few were able to move towards that choice, feeling that they had signed up to provide financially for their spouse and family and were trapped. Enviously, they watched their partners pursue new interests and goals and sometimes bitterly observed any possibilities of the realisation of their own dreams wither.

Alongside this, figures for male suicide and violence against women are on the increase. Of the 433 suicides recorded in 1997 most were men. Figures for female rape continue to rise at a time when the general crime rate is lowering. From March 1998 – March 1999 325 rapes were reported to the Gardai, up from 299 in the twelve months to March 1998. All is not well with men despite some very positive moves which may be occurring.

THE ECONOMY

The Irish economy has grown strong in the 1990s after the long recession of the 1980s, and unemployment rates are dropping steadily. The Medium Term Review 1997-2003 by David Duffy, John Fitzgerald, Ide Kearney and Fergal Shortall published by the ESRI, states 'From a position of relative underdevelopment just a decade ago, Ireland is now emerging as a modern, developed economy with a strong underlying growth potential'. The Irish economy is one of the fastest growing economies in Europe. This is emphasised by the growing number of emigrants returning – 6,000 in 1996.

In a survey published in January 2000 Dublin was identified as one of the top cities in the world in which to live. The survey covered 218 cities and evaluated 39 key quality-of-living standards in each city. These standards included factors such as political, economic and environmental issues as well as personal safety and health, education, transport and other public services. Dublin beat cities such as Boston, New York and Rome and shared its score with such cities as Los Angeles and Seattle.

At least one factor contributing to this current success is connected to changes in the circumstances for women. Irish women have traditionally been well educated but withdrew from the work force at marriage or the birth of children. Women are now entering, remaining in and returning to the workforce in greater numbers.

Everything about our economic status is improving; we are in receipt of extensive resources, educationally and materially to live our lives. Horizons widen; courses, holidays, promotions beckon. This may mean more childcare but we can afford it, or work demands it, and therefore it seems acceptable. Sure, it might be lovely for you to have a weekend away together as a couple, but will your two-year-old manage a separation of three days from you? American society shows us that there is no correlation between wealth and a willingness on the parent's part to undertake greater childcare. As people became more affluent, longer and longer hours of childcare are sought, since many other demands are introduced. In the realms of childcare, relationships and family life, money cannot be the core dimension that decides choices – the quality of life of each member of the family must be the core factor.

As an economy thrives and a society moves away from a history of struggle, the pursuit of happiness comes into central focus. The difficulty of reconciling one's pursuit of dreams with being a responsible parent can be difficult. In psychology there is a distinction made between ego syntonic behaviour and ego dystonic behaviour (where the person is troubled by their behaviour). Ego syntonic behaviour causes no such internal conflict, rather it feels in harmony with the self and one's deepest needs and desires. However, this doesn't mean that it's appropriate or 'healthy' behaviour; it only means it doesn't cause the self any pain, even if it may be causing havoc in the lives of others. The over-indulgence referred to earlier is also facilitated by increased financial gain. Because of deprivation in the parent background, it is seen as a positive factor to be able to provide a superfluous amount of clothing, food, toys, outings, activities, playstations, etc, the guide being 'We can afford it'. This often has the secondary aim of appeasing the parent's guilt; it cloaks dilemmas such as what to do when a child says she doesn't want to go to the crèche or the childminder that day or week.

CHILDREN

Almost one quarter (24 per cent) of the Irish population is aged under fifteen years. The figure has declined over the past decade, having been 29 per cent in 1986. We have the highest young population of the fifteen European union countries, where the average population of newborn to fourteen years is eighteen per cent. In the wake of the feminist movement it began to be acknowledged that children, too, were oppressed and in need of liberation. Dr Spock in the 1950s and 1960s began to place the child as a very central part of the family, and advocated listening to and respecting him/her. Slowly this attitude, backed by psychotherapy, seeped into Irish culture and became accepted as the appropriate way for children to be treated: psychologists, social workers, teachers and parents could receive training in the most effective ways to listen, respect and respond to children.

The UN Convention on the Rights of the Child was ratified by Ireland in 1992; this convention makes states which accept it legally accountable for their actions towards children. 'Encompassing the whole range of human rights – civil, political, economic, social and cultural – the Convention recognises that the enjoyment of one right cannot be separated from the enjoyment of others. It demonstrates that the freedom a child needs to develop his or her intellectual, moral and spiritual capacities calls for among other things, a healthy and safe environment, access to medical care, and minimum standards of food, clothing and shelter. The Convention charts new territory. It establishes the right of a child to be an actor in his or her own development, to express opinions and to have them taken into account in the making of decisions relating to his or her life.' This clearly illustrates the commitment of our government to further the rights of the child – a far cry from the Ireland of the 1950s where a child was expected to be seen and not heard.

In September 1999 'Children First, the National Guidelines for the Protection of Children' was published. It clearly defines physical abuse as something harmful and to be reported and includes things like shaking, but slapping and spanking for disciplinary purposes go unmentioned. In the introduction by Frank Fahy, the Minister of State with Special Responsibility for Children, he states clearly that the protection of children is everyone's responsibility: 'one important point is that everyone has a duty to protect children and that this is not simply the job of social workers and other health professionals'. Most people are clear about physical and sexual abuse, but the guidelines also speak of emotional abuse: 'emotional abuse is normally to be found in the relationship between a care-giver and a child rather than in a specific event or pattern of events. It occurs when a child's needs for affection, approval, consistency and security are not met. Unless other forms of abuse are present it is rarely manifested in terms of physical signs or symptoms.' Another significant development is the Protection for Persons Reporting Child Abuse Act 1998, which provides a statutory immunity for persons reporting child abuse reasonably and in good faith. This means that someone reporting a concern can do that without fear of repercussions.

In a ground-breaking case in January 1999 a primary school principal who pulled a boy's hair and struck him on the back of the head was found guilty of common assault. Up to 1996 and the Offences Against the Person Act, teachers had remained immune from criminal liability for physical chastisement, even though corporal punishment had been abolished by the Department of Education since 1982. Ms Fionnuala Kilfeather of the National Parents Council (Primary) put the decision in the context of Ireland's ratification of the Convention and said, 'We are pleased to see the 1996 Act being used to send out a strong signal from the state about how we expect our children to be treated'. It seems a possibility that parental physical chastisement might also be challenged under this law.

In terms of children's rights, the report from the Commission on the Family emphasised its support for the recommendation from the Constitution Review Group (1996) that a child has the right, as far as is possible, to a knowledge and history of his/her own birth parents for health, genetic and psychological reasons. People who have been adopted have struggled for years with restrictions that gave them very little autonomy in their quest for information. It is every child's right to know their parentage but since the circumstances of their birth may have been very difficult and shaming for the mother, such matters must be handled sensitively. During 1992, a boy in

Florida divorced his natural parents in order to free himself for adoption by his foster parents. Other similar cases followed in Europe and America.

Regarding psychological pressure, children are being put under more and more strain to succeed beyond their abilities. David Elkind in *The Hurried Child* speaks of 'the damage that's done when a child is hurried'. The child's own harmony is interfered with and may never again be restored. Evidence of this syndrome abounds throughout childhood but is nowhere more evident than on the child's first day at school. If parents and teachers were prepared to accept the different styles and abilities of children to separate from the parents and move into the class days and activities at their own pace, everything could be so much easier. Different possibilities could be offered to facilitate parents to remain in the classroom or close at hand. Instead, fraught and anxious parents thrust the children forward into the clutches of the equally anxious teacher. The successful entrant, whose compliance is ensured sometimes by threats or bribes, is the one who causes the least fuss and separates easiest. I recall seeing a parent run from the classroom to the bereft howls of her offspring, only to return at collection time with some much desired toy, handed over with ardent solicitude; 'Now, sure you won't cry tomorrow.'

Parents are often bolstering their own self-esteem by asking their children to be successful and highly achieving. Too frequently children are asked to fulfil their parents' dreams. Parents need to enhance their own lives and pursue their own dreams but in a mature, encompassing manner, taking account of their current responsibilities.

In an article in *The Irish Times* in March 1999 by Andy Pollak, querying the possibility of modern Irish life being damaging to children ('Kids in the fast lane today are bored to pain by learning') the principal of an elite fee-paying school with an enviable ten-to-one pupil-teacher ratio expressed his concern about the difficulties his pupils were experiencing with the current curriculum. One contributing factor mentioned was the very high expectations children have of themselves in today's affluent society. If those expectations are not met then disappointment, and possibly even disillusionment, may result. High achievers are generally more prone to disillusionment which, though a natural stage of development, may be psychologically damaging if encountered too early in life.

PARENTING

Parenting too has changed and is ever more demanding. Calls to 'Parentline' from distressed parents seeking assistance were up by twenty per cent in 1997. The Taoiseach, Bertie Ahern, at the launch of their report acknowledged that 'Irish society is changing more rapidly now than in any other time in our history. The role of the parent is where the impact of change is most strongly felt'.

Parents who work outside the home may experience a dual strain, wishing to spend as much time as possible with their children while also seeking to advance their careers. Work pressure for parents tends to be at a maximum when childcare duties are most demanding. Research indicates that men and women fight more about housework and children than anything else. The Parental Leave Act, which came into force in December 1998, may ease things somewhat. Both parents are entitled to fourteen weeks unpaid leave before a child is five years old. Already employers are looking to their work forces and anticipating its impact. However, a survey published in October 1999 by the Department of Justice, Equality and Law Reform indicated that only fourteen per cent of the state-sponsored organisations surveyed afforded paternity leave.

At the National Forum on Early Childhood Education held in March 1998 the National Parents Council (Primary) called for parenting classes to be taught at second-level schools. Given the fact that teenage parents are getting younger and younger (ten per cent of all births outside marriage in 1997 were to girls under fifteen), this seems indeed a necessity. Other experts, such as criminologists, are also strongly recommending parenting courses, as numerous studies have shown that parent training can be effective in reducing later delinquency. Professor John Farrington of Cambridge University, the author of a number of books on criminology, recently recommended a programme of investment in parenting during pregnancy and in the first years of a child's life.

Penelope Leach, a well-known author and child psychologist, has recently begun to speak about a new problem for parents. First time mothers are now much less confident and at ease with their babies, since their world has involved so much more than the preparation for motherhood, and also because of the breakdown of the extended family connections whereby females were kept in contact with babyhood throughout their teenage years and early twenties. Mothers can be left feeling isolated, unskilled and vulnerable in the first months and, because of experiences predominantly of competence in their lives, may feel unable to share their feelings, even with their partners.

Early in 1998, the dictum of 'quality time' by which many working parents lived was debunked. Diane Ehrensaft, Professor of Psychology at the Wright Institute, Berkeley, California, published research which indicated the damage it might cause. Some children were growing up anxious and pressurised, unable to be happy unless the focus was on them. 'There has been this assumption that if you substitute so-called quality time for quantity time then the children will be okay. It is not. We are giving children a double identity which isn't healthy,' she says. Parenting cannot be squeezed in between the meeting and dinner; important discussions don't just happen, quality time occurs within quantity time. So often I've observed that significant communications from children occur while doing insignificant things together- it just gets said in passing and you could almost miss it. In fact, if you ask directly you won't usually receive much information. Children also just need to know you're there, available if required, but otherwise invisible. So, ideally, people need time to think through the emotional requirements of parenting and to be flexible, open to change, willing to learn and admit their shortfalls.

Susan Walzer in 1996 identified the 'mental labour' that is a substantial part of parenting, which again is predominantly the domain of females and difficult to legislate for. It involves the interpersonal work that is a vital part of parenting, such as wondering and worrying about the child and her needs as well as overseeing a lot of practical details such as who needs new clothes, etc. This emotional mental work has been the glue of relationships, the sustaining input expected of women. 'Only when the work of thinking about the baby is shared can new fathers claim to be truly equal participants,' she claims. 'Mental labour,' as everyone knows, is not something you begin and end, it becomes a part of you, it keeps you tuned in to your children's needs and helps keep them feeling safe and secure.

Active parenting is increasingly demanded for longer periods as the length of time children stay in their parents' care has increased. Adult children attending third level institutions either live at home into their twenties or need to be financially supported to live elsewhere. In France, where almost two-thirds of young people enter higher education, this has become something of a phenomenon. Child benefit has just recently been extended to the age 22 to meet the financial demands of the 'stay at home' generation.

FAMILIES

Family size, in Ireland, has halved over the past 25 years. As described by the UN International Year of the Family in 1994, a family is any parent/child relationship. The traditional idea of family being a married couple and children has changed. Marital breakdown, the fall in the rate of marriage and births and the rise in births outside marriage have contributed to this change. According to the 1996 Irish census there were 31,296 family units consisting of cohabiting couples, 40 per cent of which had children.

Families, in theory, should be nurturing, stable units

conferring rights and responsibilities on its members but this is not always the case. Family units now change and reorganise themselves frequently; children find themselves living with other children who are no relation to them, or find themselves with new 'siblings' without being given adequate time to accommodate such a change. We have exchanged large families for disparate families; fathers and mothers can be parents to more than one family. Different combinations of families exist – a person forms a relationship and has children with that partner, while attempting to become a part-time parent to children from an earlier relationship.

Most people agree on the benefits of being able to leave a bad relationship, but the research regarding children is less convincing. Changes in children's living environments, including separations and new unions, need to be carefully negotiated. Understandably this proves to be a mammoth task when the separating partners are angry and perhaps vengeful towards each other, or when a besotted new couple is in joyous celebration of their union. An enduring amount of maturity is required from the adults concerned to withstand the difficulties and advance matters.

The position of fathers, divorced, separated or otherwise, continues to be considered. John Waters persistently champions the rights of men, and particularly fathers, in *The Irish Times*. The organisation Parental Equality was set up eight years ago, 'to promote shared parenting and joint custody following relationship breakdown'. The advantage of joint parenting and joint custody following the breakdown of the relationship, it claims, exists for the child, father, mother and extended family and it helps to ease the stress of the separation for everyone involved. The cohabiting father is still without automatic rights as a parent, but under the Children Act 1997 an unmarried father may acquire guardianship rights by agreement with the mother by making a joint statutory declaration. The amount of child access afforded to divorced fathers is often seen as punitive and insufficient to provide for a strong bonded relationship with a child.

In Sweden, the basic rule is that legal custody is split between the parents. In *Changing Fathers?* McKeown, Ferguson and Rooney, in querying whether father's rights and responsibilities are adequately promoted in Irish law, state, 'Taking all the evidence we have received here into account, we believe that the courts should have a discretionary as opposed to a mandatory power to award joint custody. In our view joint custody is the appropriate option for the court to consider, unless the evidence and the circumstances suggest otherwise.'

Relationships between men and women have been steeped in discussions of power since the 1960s and it has frequently been suggested that the state of marriage is an oppression for women. In an interesting study on cohabitation carried out in Britain by Dr Susan McRae, she found that parents who had been living together for a long time appeared to be no more egalitarian than married parents. Discussion of power issues between parents and children have been brought to the fore by the disclosures of parental physical and sexual abuse and the silence heretofore surrounding such crimes has been broken. The Irish Society for the Prevention of Cruelty to Children (ISPCC) and the Children's Rights Alliance work to inform children of their rights. Overall there is a move towards consultation and negotiation between parents and children regarding all matters pertaining to the life of the child.

MARITAL BREAKDOWN

For most of this century, Ireland was unusual among western countries with its low marriage rate and high marital fertility. In the 1970s and 1980s marriage reached its highest figures with people marrying younger; the average age for women was 24 and for men 25. The number of marriages has dropped steadily since the late 1980s until early 1998. Since then, according to the Central Statistics Office, marriage has been once more on the increase. Marriage as a rite of passage into a committed relationship has become a confused issue. Frequently now young couples live together for a prolonged period, buy a home together, perhaps have a child, then get engaged and after a further lengthy period, get married. Clearly old and new concepts are floundering around together, creating a very confused idea of when people actually enter a committed relationship. Is it when they decide to live together, to have a child, to buy a house, or when they buy a ring and announce their intention to marry, possibly after all of the aforementioned? Even with this prolonged period of pledges prior to marriage, marital breakdown is increasing. The 1996 Irish census indicated that 1,356,600 people described themselves as married and a further 272,200 who had been married were now either widowed or separated. 5,000 people have applied for divorce in the last two years and 2,700 have had their divorces granted. Marriage is still the experience of the majority of people but the number of children born outside marriage to either single women or cohabiting couples is increasing. In 1997 the figure was 13,900, over 25 per cent of the total birth rate of 52,300. The dramatic increase in marital breakdown emerged prior to the introduction of divorce. In the United States half of all marriages end in divorce and 40 per cent of children are affected by divorce. In Britain the figure is between one-third and a quarter.

Women are more likely to formally end the marriage through petitioning for separation or divorce, while the 1991 census showed that desertion also was more likely to be a female experience; 71 per cent of those who were deserted were women. In her book *Emerging Voices*, on women in contemporary Irish society, Pat O'Connor speaks of this phenomenon: 'The high levels of desertion in Ireland, and their predominantly male character ... can be seen as reflecting the inability of some men to deal either with what they see as the emotional demands in this situation, or the emotional consequences of its disruption.'

To form and maintain a successful relationship nowadays, an ability to communicate and negotiate practical as well as emotional difficulties is required. Inadequacies and problems arise where prior life stages have not been well managed, such as a move from home or entering third level education. An intimate relationship offers a site for all the old ghosts to revisit. People enter relationships thinking all will be well now they've found the perfect partner. The 'perfect partner' may be someone who will in fact encourage those old ghosts one was only too willing to believe were buried, now to be recreated, alive and vibrant, in a different setting. Fuelled by media images of love being enchanting, thrilling and above all appeasing, a couple encountering such difficulties may feel they are wrong for each other. Instead they are being offered an opportunity to negotiate aspects of their personality which have remained immature and perhaps infantile.

Intimate relationships between men and women no longer work where women take all the responsibilities for the emotional life of the relationship. In this kind of arrangement one works around the other person but little real engagement occurs. Such couples rarely have arguments or disagreements and might be lured into the illusion that they get along very well. However, all of the undeclared difficulties are there and the backlash can be found when one partner just coldly ends the relationship or commences an affair. It takes a secure relationship to be able to weather the storms of interaction and still find sufficient warmth and connection with each other for the relationship to be a reassuring place of comfort and solace.

Many women and men are seeking peer marriages, where childminding and financial responsibilities are equally shared. Children are becoming the mutual responsibility of both parties. For such couples, the necessity for work to encompass a relationship, children and family life is also becoming a reality. Two people now must be responsible for the emotional life of the relationship and family and above all the couple must be solid, supportive friends to each other.

Adhering to an ideology of romantic love is likely to bring disillusionment, disappointment and eventual dissolution of the relationship. In a study entitled 'Peer marriage: how love between equals really works', P. Schwartz identified four factors which contribute to marital stability: a) Having less than a 60/40 split on chores and child minding; b) Equal influence over important decisions; c) Equal financial control; and d) Each person's work given equal importance in their life plans. In essence, she is describing a balanced equal partnership where both parties respond to high demands made of them and each person's needs are respected.

LONE PARENTS

Ireland has the highest number of lone parents in the EU, including widowed parents, those who are separated and parents who are not married. According to the 1996 census over one in six families is headed by a lone parent, 130,000 out of 806,800. The majority of lone parent families, more than four in five families, are headed by women.

As stated in the Medium Term Report 1997-2003 published by the ESRI, marriage in the past played an important part in determining female participation in the work force. Now it is the presence of children rather than marriage which has become the crucial factor in determining participation, and the participation rate for single women with children is below that of married women with children. In 1995 under 30 per cent of lone parents were at work. Lone parent families face a greater risk of poverty than other families. More than 50 per cent of lone-mother families in Australia, the US and Canada live below the poverty line. Discussion abounds about the lone mother and childcare, stating that if childcare was better organised and less costly lone mothers would choose to work outside the home. Undoubtedly more lone mothers would seek employment, but some would still wish to parent full-time and as a state, we need to ask is this feasible?

Lone parents are of course a disparate grouping, including teenagers who have become parents and may still be pursuing educational goals or have not yet received adequate training for work. This grouping may initially continue to live at home with their parents and in time move out or marry. There are also divorced or widowed parents who are parents of more than one child, and those who have chosen to parent alone.

A recently formed pioneering group of fifteen-to-nineteen-year-old school-going mothers published their annual report in August 1999, highlighting their needs and the obstacles they face. 'As education holds the key to breaking dependence on the state in the long term, it is imperative that every assistance is given to encourage people who are in this situation to become independent and create for themselves and their children a decent lifestyle and life chances,' the report states.

Lone parent families face a greater risk of poverty than other families. In 1995 under 30 per cent of lone parents were at work, and the majority of lone parents depend on social welfare as their primary or only source of income. In December 1996 there were almost 70,000 lone parent families receiving weekly income support payments from the Department of Social, Community and Family Affairs. Unmarried parents are required, under recent regulations, to seek maintenance for their child from the other parent if they apply for social welfare payments. Research has shown that children of single parents are particularly liable to be admitted to the care of health boards between the ages of two and five years. Lone parents in countries such as Denmark or Sweden, with a high degree of gender equality and high rate of participation for married women, are more likely to be in employment and less likely to be poor. In some of these countries the children are awarded priority in access to childcare, which seems wise given that there is only one parent, not two, to accommodate the child's minding.

Some women choose to parent alone and not involve a father in the child's life; this number seems to be on the increase. This is further facilitated by the existence of sperm banks. As an American child recently explained to me, 'I don't have a dad, I've got two moms and a donor'. Interestingly, Swedish law recognises the right of the child to both its parents; anonymity in connection with donation of sperm is not allowed. In cases of adoption in Ireland, the unmarried father cannot usually prevent the adoption of his child or adopt the baby himself, against the will of the mother, even though the Adoption Act 1998 decrees that steps must be taken to consult with the father. In a book published in February 1998, *Baby wars: Parenthood and Family Strife* by Robin Baker and Elizabeth Oram, the futility of fatherhood as a concept was outlined. Baker is an evolutionary biologist who claims that the notion of bi-parental care as the ultimate system is a misconception. After impregnation he sees the father's main input as financial, as human fathers have very low rates of interaction with their children. He states this with all the certainty of evolutionary history behind him!

DEVELOPMENTS IN THE WORKPLACE

Margaret Fine-Davis in 1988, in her report for the Second Joint Committee on Women's Rights, spoke of women's attitudes needing to change: 'Women need to come to terms with the unreasonable demands they are making of themselves and begin to accept that they are entitled to work which is flexible and accommodating to their needs, since the dual roles which they perform are in the interests of society as a whole.' This is still true today; women's expectations need to increase, it is a right to be a parent, and to be facilitated in the workplace.

The demand for work to be more flexible and to take greater account of family life is a feature of the 1990s. A greater balance between work and family life is being sought, but old habits die hard and many companies still demand a rigid separation between work and home. Speaking of changes which have occurred in the workplace in Britain and the United States, Jayne Bruxton, author of *Ending the Mother War*, says, 'The family-friendly workplace in its existing state will not resolve the clash between work and family'. Workers are expected to spend long hours in work and also be available for socialising in work-related events after working hours.

Although the participation of married women in the Irish workforce is increasing – the total number rose by 40 per cent between 1987 and 1993 and in 1993 married women accounted for 50 per cent of all women at work – it is still lower than other European countries. A number of family-friendly work initiatives have been set in motion in recent years: part-time working, flexitime, job sharing, career/employment breaks, extended leave, term-time working and of course the Parental Leave Act 1998. Women are more likely to avail of these options and men continue to maintain a strong attachment to full-time, continuous work. Generally this means that women carry the stress and burden of trying to remain the main carer whilst maintaining a career. As Swiss and Walker wrote in *Women and the Work/Family Dilemma: How Today's Professional Women are Finding Solutions*, 'For twenty years now working mothers have done all the accommodating in terms of time, energy and personal sacrifice that is humanly possible and still they have not reached true integration in the workforce'. A small example of this is the fact that women are guilty of a greater level of absenteeism from work; usually this is due to a child being ill, but the employee will often have to claim illness herself in order for her absence to be seen as valid. Nevertheless the Parental Leave Act 1998 does give employees limited time off for family emergencies caused by accident or illness. This leave is paid and is separate from parental leave. It is limited to a maximum of three days in each twelve-month period or five days in each 36-month period. In cases of adoption it used to be the practice that the adopting mother was required to give up work. Adoption requirements have now changed. The Adoptive Leave Act 1995 granted leave from work of a minimum of ten weeks (and up to four weeks at the request of the employee) and the right to return to work.

Men who opt for career breaks generally do so for education or career reasons while women usually do so on family grounds. In the Equality Authority report 'Introducing Family-Friendly Initiatives in the Workplace', Hugh Fisher states, 'up to now, most men have not accepted, and have not been expected to take on, joint responsibility for running the household ... greater emphasis on men's roles within the home, particularly in relation to shared responsibility for parenting, is essential to equality both within the home and the workplace'. The report also refers to the 'double shift' syndrome whereby working mothers are still expected to do all or most of the housework.

Only three per cent of top management positions are occupied by women. Predominantly, women working in a profession tend to choose positions in education or health. In the 1996 labour force survey women occupied 65 per cent of this grouping. Women hold 70 per cent of clerical positions. According to the 1999 edition of *Women in the Labour Force* published by the Employment Equality Agency, women are 'notably under-represented in some of the fast-growing sections and occupations, and within professional occupations, women are still seriously under-represented in the higher grades'. The average hourly earnings of women are just 73 per cent of male earnings. In a recent survey completed for the Minister for Justice, Equality and Law Reform (October 1999) it was found that only 55 per cent of the state-sponsored organisations surveyed had an equal opportunities programme. In relation to employment initiatives roughly half of those surveyed said that flexitime, job sharing and career breaks were available. A very encouraging outcome is that the organisations involved will be contacted to give them feedback, and those organisations who choose not to participate will also be contacted.

To reshape our working lives is harrowing; it involves appraising our priorities and values and will only take place in an environment where personal change is occurring. We may feel alone and isolated in our choices. To have the strength to stand for what we believe, while at the same time fearing we're going to be passed over for promotion or seen as insufficiently committed to our jobs, is frightening. But if personal change is occurring at both staff and managerial level then groundwork is being prepared for such changes. Otherwise lip service may be paid to the options outlined but little true appreciation of their value or necessity will exist.

THE ROMAN CATHOLIC CHURCH

From the late 1980s the position of the Catholic Church in Ireland has been changing. In May 1992 it was revealed, in a scandal which rocked the state, that the Bishop of Galway, Eamonn Casey, had fathered a child. His lover, Annie Murphy, then published a book giving explicit details about the affair. The 1990s saw further revelations of deceit, corruption, sexual abuse and physical violence within the Catholic Church. As a result the Irish population became increasingly disillusioned; some distanced themselves but many continue to identify themselves as Catholics while being very critical and dismayed. In a European Values Study by Hornsby-Smith and Whelan (1994), it was shown that 96 per cent of Irish respondents identified themselves as belonging to a church and 97 per cent of those were Roman Catholic. Similarly an MRBI poll (1998) reported that 92 per cent identified themselves as Catholic. Research also has found that the Irish were more likely than their European counterparts to believe in heaven, sin, life after death and the existence of a soul. While the majority continued to identify themselves as Catholic, the lack of confidence in the church also emerged in research. Hornsby-Smith & Whelan (1994) found that the majority of Irish Catholics (58 per cent-66 per cent), similar to their European neighbours, did not have confidence in the church's ability to deal with the problems of family life, moral problems, the needs of the individual or the social problems of the country. Again a study in 1993 (Noonan) showed that women were going against the church's teaching on contraception – 84 per cent of women aged 17-49 had used contraceptives. Yet women were also highest in the figures for church attendance, especially those who worked full-time in the home, were over 40 years of age, lived in rural areas and had less than a third level education.

All about me I hear discrepancies between people still identifying themselves as Catholic, yet not being very active within that church or adhering to its beliefs and not respecting the ministering agents of that church. As a society, we have been told how to behave and think by a church and in return have received reassurance about an afterlife. Those structures are now disintegrating and people are being required (or are choosing) to think for themselves and inspect their own morality. Unfortunately, because of our history of being led, this aspect of the Irish psyche is not very well developed. People feel frightened in the face of such a void and seek answers. In his book, *Progress and the Invisible Hand*, Richard Bronk, in speaking of the age of enlightenment, describes how the period of transition from a religious to a secular age is characterised by the fact that 'individual conscience is still schooled in the lessons of guilt ...' This is apparent in the influx of new theories and religions from the east. Many philosophies carry strong rules and regulations by which to live and how one can be 'saved'. Visiting gurus now frequent Ireland at a staggering rate – everything Irish, religious and Catholic is seen as bad and beliefs pertaining to other times and cultures are wholeheartedly embraced. New age theories are responded to with childlike ferocity and certainty; little true spiritual or psychological growth will be achieved. This is dangerous; we have a very long history of spirituality within our culture which may never have been successfully harnessed by any Irish church. Perhaps we should look more closely to ourselves and to those other cultures (and ask how successfully such beliefs have been implemented there) before we innocently embrace such ideals.

As stated earlier, women have been the greatest champions of the church in Ireland, yet the Catholic Church continues to discriminate against them, thus alienating the more educated and enlightened groupings. Despite diminishing numbers of ministers, women are doggedly refused access to positions of ministry. It is merely evidence of the oppression of women that they continue to frequent a church which treats them so abominably. Were they to boycott this church, it would undoubtedly flounder without their support, and would have to succumb to their requests for inclusion.

LIFE EXPECTANCY

As life expectancy increases, so the reality of death recedes. People are living longer; life expectancy in 2025 is expected to be 85.2 years for men and 92.6 years for women. We are beginning to feel invulnerable. Ernest Becker in *The Denial of Death* speaks of the syndrome whereby death is denied through the dismissal of the impact on our lives of not facing death. By denying it, we neither fully live nor equip ourselves to face our own dying. That disavowal of death becomes more apparent as a society becomes wealthier, and an illusion of power is created. Death is intractable, we must encounter it. Becker suggests that in facing death and that shadow under which we are constantly spinning webs of deceit and delusion, we would enable ourselves to be so much clearer about what is important and worthy of attention and what is a waste of time.

People over 65 now make up 11.4 per cent of the total Irish population, but by 2025 that percentage will have risen to 17.25 percent. With that amount of people who have so much life experience and living behind them, we should have a very steady level-headed society. Mostly, we hear talk of frailty and the amount of dependents we will have, with little acknowledgement given to the resources which these older people can provide.

The concept of retirement will need to be re-explored. For a time, the retirement age was lowering, but if people are going to live longer and be healthy in their older years, it may no longer be sensible to consider retirement at 60 or 65 years of age. People may indeed retire from one job to take up another. At present, a strong percentage of successful small businesses are set up by people who've taken early retirement; a) with financial demands decreasing they can now pursue an interest without the main concern being monetary return and b) they now have the confidence to try something which fear of failure in younger years would have prevented them attempting. Overall, older people will have to remain an integrated grouping in society instead of experiencing the kind of ghettoising we see now. It is suggested by groups working against ageism that the retirement age may rise to 80. The population over 65 will themselves need to be aware of the talents and resources they harbour and be willing to share them, hopefully in a cherishing environment.

A society can be measured by how it treats its young and its elders, two groupings who are seen as economically unproductive. If policies are economically driven, then the grouping who are the most productive will be the most cared for and respected. Obviously such a society will be discriminatory and non-inclusive and is not the society we need for the future. Stephen Covey, a successful management consultant, proposes an integrated, holistic approach to life, work and living and feels we will not survive if we don't shift our goals to a more caring, inclusive society.

Chapter 3

CHILDCARE

Ireland has the highest number of children per family in the EU, according to the Commission on the Family published in 1998. According to a survey published in July 1999 by the Irish Congress of Trade Unions, childcare and the need for a family-friendly working environment have replaced low pay as the most important concerns of women workers, though grievances about pay are, of course, still significant.

Our childcare system fares badly by comparison with other European countries. Our maternity leave is a meagre fourteen weeks of paid leave, then three months of unpaid parental leave. Mothers working outside the home are returning to work before any stable period of breastfeeding has been established. Babies are thereby prevented from having a lengthy period of bonding and ease with their mother. Most mothers who return to work experience a lot of difficulty in trying to breastfeed. Then the parents set out to find good childcare and enter the labyrinth of privately-run childminding services. Those who are fortunate find capable and trustworthy long-term minders, those who are not shift and change from system to system, heaving a sigh of relief when the child finally enters the school system. Our childcare system is appalling. For a country which has enshrined in its constitution a commitment to family life and children, we have a lot to live up to. The life of the mother who works outside the home is still a punitive one, since she, as research shows, is the one who predominantly carries the burden of responsibility for caring for the child. Our society insidiously still reveres the woman who stays home full-time to care for the children, and is reluctant to acknowledge that this type of family structure is diminishing.

Childcare policies cannot be simply about finding services which will care for these children while their parents are free to work; it must take account of the children's needs for their parents and acknowledge that parents exhausted from heavy work schedules cannot parent well. There are 244,700 children under school going age. 77,000 of these are cared for away from their parents for some part of the week, therefore one-third of pre-school children regularly attend nurseries, crèches or child-minding services. Childcare provision takes a variety of forms – sessional services, full-day care, childminders, drop-in centres, the early start programme, after-school care, parent and toddler groups and au pairs. Play-groups offer care and education to children aged three to five years. Approximately 80 per cent of playgroups are privately run and home-based. There are 254 Irish language playgroups, the Naionrai, set up by An Comhchoiste Reamhscolaiochta Teo. A part-time pre-school service is provided for children aged three to six years by the Montessori schools, of which there are approximately 500, and the Steiner Kindergartens, of which there are twelve. Nurseries/crèches provide group care for children aged from three months. According to official figures, in July 1998 there were approximately 400 nurseries, catering for approximately 13,000 children between newborn to six years. The average number of places per centre was 42 and the majority of children were cared for full-time.

Childminders provide a varied service and the Childcare (Pre-School Services) Regulations 1996 permits one childminder to care for up to six children. There are no figures available on the number of childminders in Ireland. Some families use au pairs to provide childcare services. In 1979 the Council of Europe drafted a European agreement on au pair placements, but Ireland has not ratified this agreement.

The Early Start Pre-school Programme, set up in 1994, is a

one year pre-school programme for newborn to three years in disadvantaged communities. The social benefits of early education for children from disadvantaged areas have been well documented. I believe such groups certainly have a value yet that value, may not lie in the acquisition of skills but rather in the organised care and attention given, which naturally is beneficial. Sources such as Penelope Leach and David Elkind believe that children themselves are sufficiently capable of determining what they need and wish to learn, and interference at too early a stage can be an intrusion. Both express concerns about formalising education too early. Parents frequently are delighted to boast about what their two-or three-year-old can do, or is learning, but these experts suggest that all children are avid and eager learners and only ever require assistance or guidance, not leading. Elkind, in his new book *Miseducation – pre-schoolers at risk*, says the ever-increasing trend to formalise children's education earlier and earlier can have serious negative repercussions. He claims that long-term studies show that formal education from an early age creates anxious children who carry this anxiety on into teenage years.

Parent and toddler groups offering play are established in many communities. Such groups are valuable in that they offer the parent and child companionship. The parent gets to meet other parents and the child enjoys the opportunity to play with, or in the vicinity of, children of similar age. Drop-in crèche centres exist as part of customer services in many shops and shopping centres. Toddlers can best utilise such services if they return on a regular basis. They can get to know the minder and look forward to spending a short time there regularly. However, leaving babies in such situations is not wise. Babies need greater security in their minding arrangements. The time would be too short and infrequent to build any kind of rapport between minder and baby.

Some workplaces operate crèche facilities. In a recent survey carried out by the Department of Justice, Equality and Law Reform, childcare facilities within workplaces were found to be very bad. Of the organisations who responded to the survey, only six per cent offered direct support and fourteen per cent indirect support. Crèches in the workplace provide a vital service to parents. Children can be visited during the day, collected earlier, and be more accessible to the parents if there is a problem. In teaching environments this could be particularly successful, since teachers at second and third level institutions do not teach continually and yet have to remain on the premises for later classes. All large companies and state-run bodies should be required to provide crèche facilities and smaller companies and work environments ought to be provided with some financial aid to include such a service.

For children under the age of two it is most common for the child to be minded either in the child's home or in the minder's home. Crèches and nurseries are most important for the ages two to four years. Figures for childminding for school-going children under twelve, who are cared for after school or during the holidays, are less accurate but guess estimates suggest a figure of over 100,000. The demand for childcare services is at an unprecedented high and is expected to increase. The primary reason for seeking childcare is where the mother is working full-time or part-time outside the home, but sixteen per cent of mothers who work full-time in the home also avail of this service. Tony Fahy stated in Budget Perspectives published by the ESRI, 'Data on the usage of paid childcare in Ireland indicate that the dominant form of childcare provision is the childminder based either in the childminder's home or the child's home, rather than the formally organised crèche or kindergarten. Such home based paid childminding is likely to be more flexible and less costly to parents, partly because much of it is carried out in the black economy, but it is also less subject to regulation and of more uncertain quality, so that its prevalence in the Irish system of childcare provision is a matter of some concern from a number of points of view.'

The case of the British au pair Louise Woodward, who was initially found guilty of murdering baby Matthew Eappen but had her sentence reduced to manslaughter, forced many of the issues surrounding childcare to the fore. Profound questions such as the value our society gives to childcare were raised, and people queried how someone so inexperienced and immature could have been given such a responsibility. Yet many such people are given care of young children. If you were employing someone to manage your company, just consider the amount of energy, effort and thought which you would put into his or her selection. The difference is that the person coming in to run a company will be highly financially compensated and the childminder will be paid very little. This is how childminding is valued. Following the Eappen tragedy, however, instead of the complicated issues that childcare presented being faced, anger was directed at the baby's mother, a 32-year-old doctor who had chosen to work outside the home. She was accused of neglect, but she had taken a part-time position at a hospital five minutes from her home, having passed up other prestigious appointments. Her work involved eight-hour shifts, three days a week, which in the medical world was a compromise. The targeting of this heartbroken mother showed how easily women are still blamed, even in the most agonising of circumstances. Middle-class mothers so often bear the brunt of such rage, being presented as avaricious, greedy and cold-hearted because they choose to work outside the home when they don't 'need' to. If this had been a financially struggling, working-class mother, I think the public reaction would have been much more sympathetic.

In January 1998 a nanny working in Westmeath was given a suspended sentence after hurting a baby in her care. A documentary, 'Nannies from Hell', appeared on our television screens in that same month, showing what some nannies can get up to when left solely responsible for young children. Hidden cameras revealed nannies spanking, terrorising and neglecting the children in their care.

Further court cases followed; in July 1998, a woman in England received a life sentence for murdering a baby in her care. She had concealed the fact that three of her own four children had been taken into care or adopted. In January 1999 an Australian nanny, also in England, pleaded guilty to involuntary manslaughter when a six-month-old baby died after being shaken by her. In 1999, a sixteen-month-old baby girl died in Manchester after being admitted to hospital with severe head injuries. Her babysitter, a thirteen-year-old schoolgirl, was accused of murdering the toddler. In October 1999 another British nanny, this time aged 44, was convicted of shaking a baby to death in California. She was sentenced to 25 years to life in prison, under a new law which states that anyone who assaults a child under eight, using force likely to produce 'great bodily injury', must serve a mandatory term of at least 25 years. In January 2000, a case came before the courts which indicated the seriousness with which childminding was now being viewed. A childminder who slapped the six-year-old boy she was taking care of in a public park was convicted of assault, on the evidence of two passers-by who saw her strike the child, though she denied the charge.

Of course it is not only in one-to-one care situations that children are at risk. In the *Sunday Tribune* in 1997, an investigation team claimed to have found very poor conditions in crèches visited in Ireland. Children were seen to be neglected, shouted at and left sitting in chairs for hours without stimulation. In February 2000, a case came before the Circuit Civil Court involving a five-month-old baby girl who, while the crèche attendant was out of the room tending to another baby, was beaten on the head with a wooden toy and bitten by an older child. A settlement of £15,000 was agreed.

Under the Child Care Act of 1991 which became law in 1996, nurseries, childminders and crèches must follow certain regulations, including staff ratios, safety in relation to premises and equipment, hygiene and fire safety. These regulations, though necessary, brought hardship because the government didn't put any financial supports in place to help the childminding agencies. Many small services were forced to close. Under section 58 of the Act certain people are excluded:

a) relatives caring for one or more pre-school children;
b) people caring for pre-school children of the same family;
c) those caring for not more than three pre-school children of different families.

Under the Act, all childminders are required to be registered with the health boards. Barnardos has called for all childminders to be checked out by the gardai.

Pre-school Officers have been appointed to implement the Childcare (Pre-School Services) Regulations 1996. The Eastern Regional Health Authority has appointed six teams of Pre-school Officers to regulate standards in the areas of Dublin, Kildare and Wicklow, their task being to provide 'advice, guidance and support to promote the safety, health, welfare and development of the pre-school child'. Under these regulations no physical punishment is permitted: 'a person carrying on a pre-school service shall ensure that no corporal punishment is inflicted on a pre-school child attending the service' (Part 2 number 8). Pre-school services are play-schools, playgroups, day nurseries, crèches or drop-in facilities, but childminders who cater for up to three children are excluded.

Many experts express the view that home-based one-to-one care provided by the same adult is preferable for the child under three. In a recently published book, *More Secrets of Happy Children*, Steve Biddulph upholds the view that long hours of childcare are detrimental to children growing up into healthy adults. Biddulph is a family therapist who, like many other experts in the area, is deeply concerned about what is happening with children. 'Children who go into care at two or three months of age, and stay for seven or eight hours a day, are basically spending their childhood in care,' he says. It cannot be psychologically healthy for young children to spend so much time away from their parents. It cannot be good for them to spend hours throughout their childhoods with an array of different minders, whether they be experienced crèche workers, transient au pairs or temporary short-term childminders. Grandparents, aunts and uncles are great options for childminders, provided you have a good relationship with them and confidence in their capabilities, otherwise the children get caught in the crossfire. Relatives will love the child/children and will remain part of their lives. It's traumatic for a child to bond strongly with the minder and then have that relationship terminated without warning. This will lead to a syndrome of near-institutionalisation. Children brought up in institutions, away from the care of one or both parents, learn to accept love, care and attention from whoever is available to care for them. Innovative practices have been implemented in recent years for children in care whereby individual carers are allocated to specific children, thereby attempting to facilitate the one-to-one bonding necessary for healthy psychological development.

The major problem for parents who choose to have a minder in the home is that the adult carer is without supervision and the younger the children, the less capable they are of indicating if there's a problem. Regulations can be implemented for crèches and childminding facilities but it proves more difficult to supervise what goes on in the home. American and occasionally British parents have employed the use of hidden cameras or private detectives to investigate either the childminder in the home or the activities of the person in their time off. If you are already this doubtful about the competence of your childminder, wouldn't it be better to let the person go? To employ such extreme measures means that you have grave reservations, surely serious enough grounds for terminating the employment, even if you are wrong.

Childminders may present themselves a particular way when dealing with another adult, but in their relations with children behave neglectfully or even cruelly. There is no accountability, as the child cannot tell, or if he is verbal and can communicate his unhappiness, the childminder may still give a different interpretation of the circumstance. Parents who feel that the most preferable situation would be to have the child minded in the home may not choose that because of these fears. In communal minding situations other children and other workers can serve as a deterrent to such abuse.

It requires incredible skill and patience to be a childminder but it is particularly difficult if the minder feels isolated and lonely. Childminders I spoke to felt unhappy with their general circumstances. Many loved their job but felt they probably wouldn't stay in it long term because of the low financial remuneration. Others, who equally liked the work, felt they wouldn't stay with that particular job because of the demands of the parents. Most agreed it was much easier to negotiate salary increases or other requests within a communal minding situation rather than within the home. Occasionally parents who employ childminders in the home can have wildly exaggerated expectations of how much can be done. Mostly, childminders felt they performed a very necessary job well without receiving much gratitude.

The National Women's Council of Ireland's policy is that 'all parents have the right to affordable, accessible quality childcare'. They are seeking a) tax relief even where only one parent is working outside the home and b) a tax allowance of £5,000 for home-based childminders to bring them into the formal economy, and they have called for urgent action by the state to provide a national childcare policy framework. The NWCI is committed to shifting responsibility for childcare from the individual woman to a public responsibility on the part of the state. A study conducted on behalf of NWCI by the Isis Research Group in Trinity looked at the EU funded NOW projects (new opportunities for women). From a feminist perspective it asks what needs to change within our economic systems so that all women can become economically independent agents.

Another formidable women's organisation, the Irish Countrywomen's Association, has called on the government to provide tax relief for childcare costs and give incentives to employers to provide crèche facilities. It sees the lack of childcare as a fundamental barrier to women entering the workforce. It put forward ten recommendations:

1) Increase in child benefit and statutory care funding for

childcare;

2) Opening up potential areas of employment;

3) Funding for ongoing in-service training and standard-ised accreditation system;

4) Enhancement of community employment schemes;

5) Accessibility of information;

6) Guaranteed percentage of EU structural funding to be allocated to childcare;

7) Integrating services and responding to experiences on the ground;

8) Giving value to caring work;

9) Encouraging new models of work participation;

10) Closing the gap to achieve equal opportunities.

A coalition of six groups, called 'Childcare 2000 Campaign', presented a submission to the Irish government in October 1999. They want an increase in child benefit, but also they want a 'Parents' Childcare Payment' to be paid to parents for each of their children. Category A would include children up to five, and category B would include children aged six to fourteen years; a higher payment was proposed for the younger grouping.

Discussions pursued formally and informally suggest the most desirable childcare arrangements, but too often even the most discerning parents are forced to compromise on financial grounds. Childcare costs about £50 per week, nurseries average about £60-£70, live-in nannies £120-£130, nannies working in the home £140 and au pairs, £40 pocket money for a 35-hour week. Parents need to be able to choose the service they want, in confidence and safety, and not find themselves in a position where it doesn't make economic sense for them to work. In the *Sunday Times* magazine in March 1998, it was suggested that London mothers would need to be earning £40,000 per annum in order to afford a nanny, and even then the mother might end up with little more than the nanny herself! In Ireland Dr Fahy of the ESRI, speaking in June 1999, foresaw crèche charges increasing to £150-£180 a week. A chain of purpose-built nurseries called 'Circle of Friends' was due to open in December 1999.

Top quality care, it was claimed, would be available for £120 a week for a toddler, with the cost being slightly higher for a baby.

According to Bernard Feeney of Goodbody Economic Consultants, a conservative estimate suggests that 40,000 additional childcare places will be needed by 2011. Childminding cannot continue to be represented as a service anyone can provide, or as a filler-in before an awaited career is pursued, or as an easy way to make money. Childcare salaries have in fact risen by approximately 50 per cent in the last year, due to the high demand for childcare services. To safeguard the needs of everyone involved and encourage long-term commitment, it is imperative that it receive the status of a viable chosen career, paying a fair wage.

Include in this equation the position of the au pair, who is young, often has meagre childminding experience, is with the family only for a specific duration, is separated from her own family and support structures and is paid very little. Yet she can be given serious childminding responsibilities very soon after arrival. One can see how something as horrific as the story of Matthew Eappen can occur. I believe that rarely should an au pair be required to spend unsupervised time with children. Ideally, they could provide a service with a parent in the house and then extend this to brief outings, etc. Providing long hours of childcare alone with children should be out of the question.

In today's climate of rising prices and increased costs, economic reasons continue to be cited as the primary reason for female employment outside the home. However, in a culture where the number of married women employed has only recently increased, it may be important to remember that women go out to work for many reasons, not just economic, though that is of course an important factor. They work to feel competent, have experience of community, boost their self-esteem and be productive; in brief, for reasons of personal fulfilment. Margaret Fine-Davis, in 'Women and Work in Ireland' in 1983, explored the relationship Irish women have with work. This report drew three important conclusions:

a) employment met many important needs for women such as companionship, fulfilment and a sense of accomplishment;

b) employment offered protection against ill-health, particularly depression;

c) that even if women had no financial need to work they would be unlikely to give up their jobs.

Other European countries have had to face the problems we're encountering and we can learn a lot from their experience. A recently published book *Women, Work and the Family*, edited by Evelyn Mahon and Eileen Drew of Trinity College Dublin and Danish academic Ruth Emerik, brings together a range of contributions dealing with the reconciliation of the family and working life in EU countries. Some aspects of France's comprehensive childcare systems are encouraging, particularly a non-taxed, non-means-tested allowance introduced in the 1980s of over £300 per month, paid for up to three years to a parent who discontinues employment to take care of a child or children under three. Half a million parents are currently availing of this allowance, reducing the proportion of women with children under three who continue to work from 69 per cent to 55 per cent.

Equally promising is the Finnish system, where all childcare is subsidised and regulated by the state and 82 per cent of mothers of children aged between seven and twelve work outside the home. Generous parental leave allows for the child to be cared for at home up to the age of three. Fathers get six to twelve days paternity leave at the time of birth, and 48 per cent of them take it.

Overall, I favour the system operated in Sweden where most adults are encouraged, or perhaps more accurately expected, to work. It has taken more than 30 years to build their welfare system but they truly seem to address themselves to the issues of equality, family life and child welfare. Parents are not put in the position of choosing between parenting and having a career; they are facilitated in both. Children's needs for both parents are recognised and men and women are deemed equally responsible for the well-being of their children. Childcare is state-funded but not necessarily state-run and this is only one aspect of their childcare programme. Paid parental leave, which can be taken by either parent, provides for up to eighteen months leave per child, while paternity leave of two weeks enables both parents to have time together with the baby. It is the male partner who takes parental leave in about 30 per cent of families. Parents are entitled to take days off (90 per year) for family reasons. A six-hour working day is the entitlement of parents whose children are under eight years. Combine this with flexitime and it is possible for parents to work in such a way as to require very little childminding during the working day.

HOW TO CREATE AN INCLUSIVE CHILDCARING SOCIETY

As a society we need to embrace certain realities:

1.) Women are entitled to work outside the home, and need to, for many varied reasons.

2.) Men can be truly loving, nurturing carers.

3.) If men are asked to become carers of the family, then women must be asked to share the financial burden of providing for the family.

4.) It is the responsibility of both parents to emotionally nurture and spend time with their offspring.

5.) All childcare services ought to be a back-up service to the care provided by parents, not the main care (as measured in hours).

6.) Young couples intending to have children need to be facilitated to consider clearly their options regarding childcare.

7.) Maternity and paternity leave must be extended.

8.) Working environments need to support parents in their parenting roles by implementing family-friendly initiatives.

9.) Childcare costs must be supplemented and crèches and childminding agencies given the required support and financial assistance to be viable, well-staffed and well-informed in the practices of childcare.

10.) Our childcare programmes need to ensure that parents can get adequate time with their children while still maintaining a career.

Our current system is unfair, harsh and punitive to women who decide to work outside the home. In general, children of parents who both work outside the home are spending too much time in childcare services.

However, it is still difficult to find equality in employment and domestic life. Even in households where both parents are employed, women's earnings may still be seen as secondary while home and caring for the offspring remains her primary responsibility. Swedish men, who are more child orientated than other males, are nevertheless reluctant to do their share of household chores; they do approximately one-third of what their female partners do. In Germany, where male participation in household chores is roughly similar, the Green Party wants to change their family law to oblige men to do their fair share of the housework. The law in question states at the moment that 'if the running of the household is left to one partner, this person is solely responsible for the housekeeping'. The Green proposal would replace this clause with a requirement that household duties be regulated. The party's spokeswoman on women's issues said in May 1999, 'If both parties are working, the 50-50 principle also has to hold true over the housework. A clear legal position is important because it can change attitudes among the public.'

Similarly, governments in other countries are taking the unequal distribution of household chores between partners seriously. In the Netherlands, Spain and Portugal, government-sponsored advertisement campaigns confront the reality of domestic life and demand that men do their fair share. In Spain, one slogan suggests, 'A man who does not share the housework is not a man!'

The Department of Education in Ireland began a pilot

project on gender and equality in a number of single-sex boys' schools in September 1998, entitled 'Exploring Masculinity'. While the overall aim of the programme is to explore masculinity and encourage an awareness of an emotional life, one hopes that such programmes will also encourage those boys, when men, to participate fully in the lives of their children and the domestic life of the family.

Numerous studies in recent years have indicated the ill-effects for children of maternal employment. It's interesting to note that the studies made on paternal employment have been undertaken with a view to exploring the negative impact of paternal unemployment. Parcel and Menaghan found in 1994 that the fact fathers work fewer hours during their children's first few years was associated with more behavioural problems, not less. In the cases of maternal employment, the risks were deemed to be greater the younger the child. Specific studies looked at the adverse effects of children being placed in day-care centres, and again the length of time the child spent there was deemed to be relevant, as was the age of the child when entering day-care. One particular study which looked at the day-care workers themselves suggested that the hours were too long for both workers and children and that hours such as 9 - 3.30pm, or part-time hours, would be more appropriate. In March 1999 Dr Elizabeth Harvey published research which concluded that the mother's employment outside the home had no significant negative impact on the children. Behaviour problems, cognitive development, self-esteem, academic achievement and other variables were investigated. In fact, in the case of single mothers and lower income families, maternal employment was seen to be beneficial. In an American study of pre-schoolers by Youngblut, Singer, Madigan Swegart and Rodgers exploring the impact of maternal employment on the mother-child relationship in single-parent families where the children had been premature and were deemed to be of low birth weight, in other words particularly vulnerable, it was found that, 'Employed mothers had more positive perceptions and provided more enriching home environments for their children. Greater attitude-behaviour consistency was associated with more positive perceptions of the parental role.' The overall conclusion was that maternal employment was a positive influence on the mother-child relationship. Such research may encourage mothers to relinquish guilt about working outside the home, but the essential and crucial question is not about maternal employment but rather how to link parental employment with childminding arrangements in order to best facilitate a quality of life for child and parent/parents, keeping to the forefront the child's needs.

In February 1999 the long awaited Report of the Partnership 2000 Expert Working group on Childcare was published. In keeping with its terms of reference, the report examined day-care facilities and services provided by people other than the parents or other relatives, which of course only addresses a small part of the overall problem.

The report found that 'compared to OECD and EU countries, the provision of childcare services in Ireland is limited ... present service provision lacks co-ordination and varies widely in quality. The Expert Working Group believes the lack of provision of quality childcare has reached a crisis level'. The report agreed a statement of twelve principles, grouped under the following headings: 1) Needs and rights of children; 2) Equality of access and participation; 3) Diversity; 4) Partnership; 5) Quality. The same working party stated that the needs and rights of children had to be the primary consideration in the strategy of childcare.

These were its recommendations:

1.) tax relief of £2,000-£4,000 per child to be given towards child minding costs;

2.) all childcare providers including childminders to be registered;

3.) childminding subsidies to be given to people on low incomes;

4.) grants and subsidies to be given to childcare providers;

5.) a pay scale to be established to reflect the value of child-care work;

6.) tax relief for employers investing in childcare;

7.) twenty per cent of childcare workers should be male.

The report estimated an increase in demand of between 25 per cent and 50 per cent between 2000 and 2011. Editorials, articles and letters debated the value, if any, of the proposals in the ensuing days and weeks. Dr Patricia Casey of University College Dublin spoke of the women who wish to stay home to take care of their children as becoming 'the untouchables in our culture' (*The Irish Times*, 4/2/1999), while lecturer and co-author of *Changing Fathers?*, Harry Ferguson, spoke of the absence of focus on the father in the resulting discussions (letter, *The Irish Times*, 12/2/1999). Garret FitzGerald (*The Irish Times*, 6/2/1999) questioned the objectives of the report and wondered, like others, whether they were predominantly economic in aim, i.e. the expansion of the workforce. While all these criticisms may be valid, the working party has brought the government into a strong engagement with the provision and supervision of childcare facilities outside of the home. Appendix 1.8 from the report, giving a summary of reports, legislation and initiatives in the area of childcare from 1980-1998, is included in the Appendix. It provides a basis from which to move forward.

We cannot seek short-term solutions, and policies regarding childcare cannot be driven by economic strategies. We must, as a society, see the value of finding flexible, inclusive solutions to our childcare issues. Childcare projects around the country, not usually associated with facilitating parents to work outside the home, but rather enabling them to simply survive by offering a much needed break from childminding or a supportive environment, remain under-funded, under-staffed and constantly in fear of having to close down. In an *Irish Times* article in October 1999 Kathryn Holmquist quite rightly argued that the Children Bill 1999, if it were to truly promote children's rights, ought to have addressed the issue of childcare. Women and men must be facilitated to work outside the home, but not at the cost of their own or their children's psychological well-being. Work environments must relate to and encompass family life in a way we haven't encountered before. A parent who wishes to stay home full-time to care for children must be financially compensated for doing that in the interim. However, one parent being acceded the right to stay home full-time for the duration of the child's childhood can mean that the other parent is granted less opportunity to spend time with the child. The consequences of one parent being assigned that position need to be seriously considered before making that the solution.

What is equally clear is that men, not just women, need to start demanding some of these things. They must begin to see the necessity of being available to parent their children and to see the enhancement it would bring to their lives. Childcare concerns have traditionally been the domain of the female; they must now become the concern of all men and women, not just those who are parents.

In Budget 2000, an allocation of £46.4 million to finance an increase in childcare facilities was conceded as well as an increase in child benefit. No childcare payments to parents were included, which angered a lot of organisations who had worked on submissions prior to the budget. For the first time, married couples were positively discriminated against. Tax assessment was individualised which meant that each person was taxed as a separate entity. Financially, it now began to make sense for both partners to be employed. The new measure was a logical step in many ways if we are to move forward, but it brought a furore of response from couples who had decided that one parent would remain at home to care for children. They now argued they were being discriminated against. Women who stayed home full-time were glorified; the insinuation was that this was the best system of childcare. The answer to our childcare dilemma is not for women to stay home full-time, long-term, but a much more comprehensive, inclusive, complex childcare programme such as those offered in Sweden and Finland.

To date, women who work outside the home have done wonderfully well, given the discrimination and lack of support they've encountered in the workplace and society and the feelings of guilt they continually harbour about what they are not providing. Let us please look forward to a co-parenting era where both parents take equal responsibility for providing the care, love, attention, minding and financial resources required to raise healthy children.

Chapter 4

PSYCHOLOGICAL CONSIDERATIONS

Any discussion of parenting, childcare and children's needs must begin with two trusted childcare experts, Benjamin Spock and Penelope Leach. Dr Spock published his challenging book, *Baby and Childcare* in 1945, and this had a profound impact on parenting and attitudes to childcare. He said (and remember it was 1945 and how advanced this thinking was) in reference to who should take care of the baby, 'Best of all is when the mother's and father's work schedules can be dovetailed so that both can work a reasonably full shift, and yet one or the other can be at home for most of the day' and later 'Another solution is for one or both parents to cut down to less than full-time jobs for two to three years ...' Extraordinarily insightful advice still cogent today, and still not utilised in circumstances where it is clearly possible. Many young couples embarking on parenthood don't consider it an option. It is more likely to be the seasoned parents who have already experienced the stresses of employing childminders who consider such a plan. Even if it can be used for the most part, and childminding services used for the time not covered, it is still worthwhile considering. It requires maturity on the part of a couple to decide to dovetail their schedules, since they will not see as much of each other as they would like and will be required to sustain their commitment to each other on a much diminished diet of bonding time. Undoubtedly, this is another good reason for taking time to establish a strong intimate relationship before having children. The latter of Dr Spock's solutions proves difficult when a couple have more than one child, as they will be agreeing to work part-time for a protracted period. Part-time employment will coincide with a time of increased financial demand, and work promotion opportunities may be diminished at a time of optimum ambition.

But by 1988, when *Parenting* was published, Spock, due to pressure from the feminist lobby and childcare providers, no longer felt that the best care was provided by parents but rather that a variety of people including relatives or childminders 'can do a satisfactory job during the parents' workdays'. He still states, however, that babies and children up to three are highly sensitive to separation, and emphasises that babies as young as six months can become depressed if abruptly separated from their main carer, i.e., the person they have bonded with.

Penelope Leach, in her most recent book, *Children First* portrays how badly we are treating our children. She convincingly argues that 'Western children are having a lousy time', and demands a reappraisal of the importance of parenting. 'Putting children at the centre of society would re-value parenting and open up new solutions to conflicts between working and caring.' She believes most societies are not putting sufficient resources into finding solutions. Her model society is Sweden which has solidly forged ahead for 30 years. My experience is that whenever that admirable childcare system is mentioned, hot on its heels comes the litany of ills existing there. Then we can all slump back into despair, confident in the certainty that only solutions with a very high price exist. But Sweden has much to teach us about taking care of our children, regardless of its other problems. Leach believes a lot of damage is done when the one-to-one relationship with the mother is interrupted too early, and she sees regular all-day separation from the parents as too difficult for a young baby. Like Spock, though, she concedes that this difficulty is lessened if there is one constant adult to attach to: an adult who is going to remain part of the child's world for some time.

One theme common to these two experts and many others

is the view that the father's role is secondary, particularly at the babyhood and toddler stage. The father is seen to fulfil his part by supporting and facilitating the mother to nurture her bond with the baby. John Bowlby, a well-known expert on mental health, stated in his seminal work for the World Health Organisation in 1951, *Maternal Care and Mental Health*, 'It is better to leave a child (under three) at home in familiar surroundings than a strange place. It is better to leave him with someone he knows and likes than a stranger. It is essential to leave him in the care of one person, who will be a mother-figure to him while you are away.' His strong belief was that the infant had a natural inclination to bond only to one person at a time. Bowlby went on to explore extensively, within the frame of psychoanalysis, the nature of the child's attachment to the mother and the difficulties arising if that attachment is interfered with or interrupted.

Winnicott also saw the father as secondary, providing protection and elbowroom for the mother to bond and enjoy the baby. He saw that enjoyment and the pleasure of the mother as an essential ingredient in contributing to the psychological health of the adult later. As Joseph Schwartz states in *Cassandra's Daughter*, 'For the last 150 years, the dominant family arrangement in the west has been the bourgeois family, currently the stereotypical middle-class nuclear family, the family with an average of 2.4 children, the father as breadwinner, the mother as homemaker. In this social arrangement, fathers, deprived of daily contact with their growing children of more than a few minutes each day, have been deskilled in their parenting role, leaving mothers to do the work of tending to the emotional and physical needs of the children as well as those of their husband.'

Psychoanalysis, one of the major agents of change of the twentieth century, was begun by Freud who strongly believed in the upholding of the traditional roles in the division of labour. In 1969 Kate Millett stated in *Sexual Politics*, that 'the three most distinguishing traits of female personality were, in

Freud's view, passivity, masochism, and narcissism ... the position of women in patriarchy is such that they are expected to be passive, to suffer, and to be sex objects; it is unquestionable that they are, with varying degrees of success, socialised in such roles.' Despite the fact that many fine female clinicians and practitioners in the early years sought to redefine the theories pertaining to femaleness and the female psyche, the patriarchal bias prevalent at the inception of psychoanalysis continued to be evident. From the 1960s on, feminism looked to psychoanalysis because of the subjective nature of its exploration and found aspects of it relevant. Numerous other psychological, analytical and therapeutic movements were birthed in the 1960s and 1970s and have served to name human experiences, hitherto unrecounted.

Notions of parenting over the last 100 years have been adamant about the central nature of the role of the mother, but since the 1970s/1980s that has begun to be challenged. As Diane Ehrensaft stated in an unpublished paper in 1971, 'We, along with other western societies, are unique in the exclusiveness of the mother's role as infant caretaker and in our emphasis on her importance, in the development of a child's social attachments.' Other options such as co-parenting have been observed and researched in recent years and the suggestion is that the infant can indeed bond with both parents and perhaps even a third person, if that person is actively responsive to the child. But more than that is excessive in the early weeks. Advocates of co-parenting even suggest that the baby may in fact get better care as instead of one exhausted mother there may be two less exhausted parents to alternate the care. Separation anxiety, which occurs from about six months on, was seen to be diminished in children where co-parenting existed, offering the prognosis that because there is more than one reliable adult to attach to, the child may be more secure. Remembering my own experience of seeing the instant rapport between my newborn babies and their father, I find the concept of fathering offered by McKeown, Ferguson and Rooney useful. They speak of an openness to strong emotional connection and communication as a prerequisite for fatherhood and urge the father to be highly active in nurturing his offspring.

One aspect of childcare which the father cannot take over is breastfeeding. And, while most experts and parents agree in Ireland that breastfeeding is best for the baby, only approximately one-third of babies are breastfed for any significant time, according to a recent study carried out by the Eastern Health Board. While a number of factors contribute to make the figure so low, one major deterrent to breastfeeding is where the woman is returning to work. Lack of facilities, irregular hours and brevity of maternity leave make breastfeeding difficult. Maternity leave in Ireland is three months while the recommended period of breastfeeding is four months. Norway, which has a 98 per cent initiation breastfeeding rate, offers a maternity leave of ten months with full pay and lactation breaks of one hour a day after the return to work.

Both Penelope Leach and Jean Liedloff question the separation of childcare from work and feel that undivided prolonged one-to-one attention may not be very good for the child. They advocate the integration of the baby into working life, espouse the notion of sibling interaction or, if a child is an only child, speak of the gains of socialising with other children and value highly the support of an extended family or community. There are many jobs where a much greater integration of babies into working life could occur but as long as we continue to separate work and childcare we won't be obliged to find solutions. Both experts unabashedly refer to the boredom, lack of mental stimulation and isolation suffered by women engaged in caring for their young children alone in their homes. Few people will disagree on the emotionally challenging nature of baby care, but in order for parents to be inspiring and stimulating long-term mentors to their offspring they need to be nurtured in many, varied ways themselves.

Babies need two primary things to grow up mentally healthy. First, they need to feel that they are a joy to the world, that their existence is celebrated, that their parents, or at least one adult, enjoy and welcome time with them. Secondly, consistent, ongoing, unhurried time with the same person or two is obligatory. This may prove difficult if the baby is being cared for in a crèche or day-care centre as staff turnover tends to be high. As Biddulph has stated in *More Secrets of Happy Children*, such children will be supremely adaptable and high on social skills, but will they have learned these to compensate for a lack of security and constancy in having the same person care for them day after day? 'This damage will be masked by an apparent gain in superficial social skills, which actually reflect the child's strategies for coping with this stressful environment, in the long term, these deficits will lead especially to problems in forming and keeping long-term relationships.' Relationship is being sacrificed all the time in the way we live. Other things are seen to be more important and the provision of stable, nurturing relationships in our children's lives is given second place. Choosing a smaller, community-based operation may prove more successful as the service, though modest, may be run by a few individuals who own the business or are very committed to it. A young baby can only sustain a negligible amount of change in childminding arrangements, and parents need to be acquainted with this fact in making their initial choice. The total amount of time parents and children spend together has dropped significantly – 40 per cent in one generation. Readers may respond with, 'It may be less but it's better', but just recall Diana Ehrensaft's research on 'quality time'.

Jean Liedloff in *The Continuum Concept*, published in 1975, talks of the interesting notion of seeing baby and childcare as a non-activity – as something that you join in the flow of, control as little as possible and generally enjoy. This type of childminding, if it ever existed, is swiftly becoming an alien concept to mothers in western countries. I believe the child needs to be in the protective loving sphere of the parent/parents or main carer, but to be left at times to investigate and amuse herself and not always have activity or play foisted upon her. The main carer needs to be available at all times to offer security and comfort, but it's important for the child to have the space to experience a sense of herself in the world. Later, children need direction and assistance in growing up, but if given these solidly-based beginnings, they are setting out from a secure starting point.

How much time do babies need?

According to most of the experts, the first days are essential for the initial and crucial bonding of the baby with the parent/parents. The child's instinctual need to bond is apparent from the beginning, and that need can be transferred to a carer who is not a parent. The presence of at least one trusted person in a subject's childhood considerably lowers the likelihood of later psychopathologies or psychosomatic disorders. The absence of such persons increases the likelihood of later pathologies. The caretaker should be familiar, sensitive to the child's needs, in tune with the child's signals and with the ability to respond promptly, capable of providing love, warmth and social stimulation for the child. The traditional view is that the child will primarily bond with the mother while the father takes a secondary and/or supportive role. However, in peer couples today, fathers involve themselves in the life of their offspring prior to their birth. They will be present for as many of the processes as possible that occur prior to the delivery date and generally will be making every effort to connect with the child. The majority of fathers take the opportunity to be present at the birth. All of these factors contribute to the father being a secure person for the child to bond with.

Clearly, the child needs both parents, if they can be available, but we are discussing here how much consistent regular time a baby must have with at least one person. If the parents wish to have a close connected bond with the child, which is enhancing and joyful for her, then obviously the time can't be too sparse, troubled, or fraught with anxiety about departures. Changeover in the minders must be calm and easy, with extra time always allowed for the unpredicted difficulty. The child's routine and time of restlessness must be observed carefully and ideally one of the parents ought to be available at those periods of difficulty. If the baby is being breastfed then that is going to determine that the majority of waking time is going to be spent with the mother, but the father can still be available for plenty of cuddles and other care-taking chores.

HOW MUCH TIME DO TODDLERS NEED?

Penelope Leach recommends that babies and toddlers need to be home based if being minded. Surroundings offer a security still at this age; familiar toys, furniture, eating utensils and particular spaces and rooms in the house all play their part. Negotiation of the routines can remain child based as there may be only one or two children to care for. Naps can be taken in their own cot or bed, within a recognisable, intimate setting. Familiar items, not just to do with the child's life, but pertaining and belonging to the parents, exist in this setting. The parents' room or bed can be used as a source of comfort; even items of clothing or other inanimate objects may serve to keep the child in connection with their loved ones. During the day, the parents will have easier access to the child by phone; a phone call by one parent to a crèche is likely to evoke every other child's desire to speak to a parent. Lunchtime visits may be a possibility by either or both parents and can be crucial in terms of maintaining daytime connection with the child. Alternatively, one parent can make the lunchtime visit while the other finishes earlier. Equally, grandparents or other relatives may take the opportunity to visit unexpectedly and will be in a position to observe how well the particular childminding arrangement is working.

If children of this age are being cared for in a group, it's important to establish that they will have a lot of individual care and attention and that their particular needs will be responded to. Developmental learning such as learning to eat from a spoon and potty training is best facilitated by the parents, and ideally should be undertaken during holiday periods where the parents can see the process through.

Toddlers need to have time everyday with their parents. It's important that the toddler's life is not one of simply being got up by the parents in the morning, spending the day with the minder, and then being put to bed again by the parents (or worse still, being in bed asleep when the parents arrive home). It's preferable that the child have a longer sleep in the day in order to gain time with the parents in the evening. The toddler can tolerate time away from the parents, and can utilise and enjoy such time, once it is with an adult that the child feels secure and safe with, but it is important to remember that she is not yet independent (though she will be moving away and trying new things) and that she still needs the security of the parents to affirm her actions and thereby herself.

HOW MUCH TIME DO PRE-SCHOOL CHILDREN NEED?

The constant need of pre-school children for their parents is diminishing. They are gaining a sense of self-determination. According to Winnicott, nursery school should not be seen as a substitute for an absent mother (I would say, parent) but rather be offered to supplement and extend that role. The pre-school child (three to four years) proclaims proudly and loudly his newly-acquired skills and abilities and shows himself keen to learn. Sometimes the well-meaning parent, anxious to provide assistance, will be disappointed when the child's keen interest disintegrates in the face of parental assistance. Fledging attempts at independent learning need to be fostered, and provision of learning forums carefully considered. Such forums ought to be non-intrusive in method and respectful of the child's own learning style. He needs to be allowed to take charge of his learning and progress at his pace. The style of learning facilitated and set up for the child at this stage will have ramifications for his future relationship with formal learning. All of these questions are relevant in the consideration of how much time the pre-school child needs with the parents.

Time away from the parents is valuable for enhancing that sense of independence, but the child must be listened to when vocalising what he is happy with and of course that may vary greatly with each child. One very successful project I implemented with my own children was that an artist friend did a weekly hour-long art class with them at home as they came to two to three years. Each child continued it for a number of years so there was always more than one child taking the class at any time, providing that essential ingredient of peer learning. One of my sons offered another innovation: he required his minder to sit down with him at a table for a period of 'work' each morning where he drew, coloured drawings, painted and generally prepared himself for school; she, on the other hand, had an experience of connecting with her own creativity and ability to teach.

It's important for this age group, as indeed for the two previous groupings, for life not to become institutionalised. Ordinary activities during the day, like going to the shops or the park or the hairdressers, teach the child about life and people, so it's not appropriate that long days are spent in a crèche or play-school environment; it is better that they are involved in a normal day's activities.

WHAT DO SCHOOL-GOING CHILDREN NEED?
Naturally, due to the wide age gap (four to twelve years), needs are going to be very varied and parents will find that their schedules will have to be modified each year in response to those needs. In general, the twelve-year-old will be more secure and spend longer hours in school than a five-year-old; this is reflected in the school timetable. However, with the provision of after-school crèche and study facilities, the school day is extending. Schools are opening earlier, with children sometimes being delivered as early as 8am; a five-year-old can now spend from 8am – 4pm in school. Another much utilised service is where a crèche provides a pick-up service from schools and children are collected by parents from the crèche as late as 6pm.

What about the delight that the young child emerges from school with, the desire to recount her achievements and whisper her foibles? Who will hear this? Who will mirror back the sense of delight and offer encouragement regarding tasks not so well done? Who will notice the glum or not so happy demeanour which requests further interaction, or simply comfort? It's important for the child to return to a one-to-one experience after the group activity of school; to a space which is hers alone, where she doesn't have to jostle to be seen and heard, a space where she can query her difficulties and understand a little. If hours pass and other activities occur in between, it may be more difficult to find the child willing to speak of her day at 7pm. A solution would be for the parent to collect the child from school, have a chat and lunch with them and then deliver them to the minder; it will make a difference to the child.

Children aged ten to twelve years may be in school legitimately for longer hours, choosing extra activities after the general curriculum ends and finishing school at 4/5pm. If this is their choice, it usually doesn't cause any problems. Sometimes, however, children are pushed into extra-curricular activities to facilitate the parents and subsequently develop an aversion to a particular sport or activity which could have been fun at a later date. A child once described to me how he had to do every extra curricular activity offered by the school, every afternoon, as his mum didn't want him home 'too early' (in this instance, the mother did not work outside the home, but valued her free time).

Children within this age group sometimes return to empty houses and spend a number of hours alone before the parents return. If the time is relatively short, say an hour or so, it may be tolerable but long hours without adult supervision are not advisable. Children may be lonely and insecure, apart from any obvious 'trouble' they may get into. Returning to a friend or a relative's house where companionship and adult supervision are available is most prudent.

WHAT DO TEENAGERS NEED?
Mostly when we talk of teenagers, the issues which come to the fore are sexuality, drink, drugs and aggression. We have had

examples of the extreme and sometimes abusive sexual behaviour our teenagers engage in and the excesses of their drug and drink intake. Teenagers, because they now have greater disposable income, are targeted by strong advertising and media campaigns. As they become an ever-increasing prey for advertising, their vulnerabilities and foibles are exploited, promising inclusion in the 'in' groupings by the use of anything from breakfast cereals to computers to clothing. A society of young people is being created whose desires are under constant manipulation.

Certainly, we know that teenagers need to be contained in their actions and behaviour and require guidance to see their way through these turbulent but exciting years, but busy parental schedules can leave gaps in supervision and space for difficulties to arise. We also need to keep in mind that their world may be changing faster than they can keep up with; their insecurities and fears need to be understood and parents must not be fooled or awed by their apparent confidence and self-reliance. They still need your care, interaction and time, but differently from before (they also may not seem so willing to receive these). A recent study carried out by Foroige, 'The Foroige Challenge 2000', found that many young people lacked self-confidence, wanted to be taken seriously by adults and wanted real friendship and trust with their peers. Of the 1,150 young people interviewed, 44.2 per cent said they would like to improve their communication skills while 37.2 per cent said they would like to have more self-confidence. Regarding relationships with other young people, 40.5 per cent said they would like true friendship and 38.1 per cent emphasised trust. Regarding communication with adults, 36.7 per cent said they would like relationships based on mutual respect, where they felt they were listened to, and a similar percentage of participants wished to be able to confide in adults. As a parent you need to know their world, and the constituents of it; informing yourself regarding their friends, interests and studies is important. Because teenagers today were born into a technological age, they are adept at computer usage and 'surfing the net'.

Some parents are so impressed by this that they give them free rein and fail to realise how bad it is for them to spend long hours in fantasy worlds, created by others.

Teenagers need to be talked to, loved and cared for every bit as much as the four-year-old, but, because they are also struggling to cut their ties of dependency to the parents and family, will want to choose such attention themselves or may resent it. The most difficult may be male teenagers, as they are grappling not just with all the changes that teenage years bring but also with trying to deny an emotional life. According to Kindlon and Thomson, authors of *Raising Cain: protecting the emotional life of boys*, 'regardless of their age, most boys are ill-prepared for the challenges along the road to becoming an emotionally healthy adult'. They talk about the 'emotional miseducation of boys', a process whereby boys are steered away culturally from their inner world, healthy attachments and emotional understanding and expression and left bereft, with a very impoverished repertoire, yet they are expected to achieve and respond adequately to the emotional needs of those around them. According to Daniel Goleman, author of *Emotional Intelligence*, the cost of emotional illiteracy is very high. In the United States teen violence has increased dramatically. Symptoms of depression affect up to one-third of all teenagers and the incidence of depression doubles for girls at puberty. Figures for eating disorders and suicide rise continually. Emotional competency in teenagers is worsening, he asserts, and under a variety of headings, utilising research already undertaken, he lists those areas:

1.) Inability to cope socially;
2.) Being anxious and depressed;
3.) Inability to pay attention or concentrate;
4.) Delinquency or aggression.

These emotional deficiencies must be addressed. 'Unless things change, the long-term prospects for today's children marrying and having a fruitful, stable life together are growing more dismal with each generation.'

HOW MUCH TIME DO CHILDREN NEED WITH THEIR FATHER?

According to Robin Baker, author of *Sperm Wars* and co-author of *Baby Wars*, children need their father very little. 'The absence of a live-in male role model seems to have little influence on the child's performance in later life,' he says. However, not everybody agrees with this viewpoint. Recent research strongly suggests that both male and female children need a male parent to an equal extent, but in different ways. A document for the European Commission Childcare Network, 'Men as carers of children', describes the complementary roles played by fathers in the development of boys and girls. What is true is that fathers spend very little time with their offspring. Some modern fathers spend as little as 45 minutes each week interacting with their children. The results of an EU survey of twelve states (including Ireland) carried out in 1994 by the European Community Household Panel showed that 32 per cent of men spent less than two hours a day with their children. Men when questioned do not always seem able to understand the reality of the situation. A. Burgess, in *Fatherhood reclaimed, the making of the modern father*, found that self-reports by fathers on their involvement and interaction with children were not always reliable. 'Because average levels of father involvement are so low, any father who does more than a very little can be rated 'highly involved' by himself, his partner – and even by researchers. Three hours a day is the figure quoted for even the most active fathers in industrial society.' In *Changing Fathers?* by McKeown, Ferguson and Rooney, research is quoted to support the theory that fathers being involved with their children has a positive impact. Men are moving into closer interaction with their children; perhaps it isn't happening fast enough to satisfy either women or children, but it is happening. The essential question is not whether or not they should or whether or not it makes a difference, but rather what do the children want/need?

Children who have had substantial time with their fathers early on continue to seek that and if it changes will voice their dissatisfaction. The children who say it doesn't matter or make a difference to the quality of their lives usually have not had it. It's a question of neither party, child nor father, knowing the richness of that relationship until they've actively engaged in it. Then they usually want more and eventually find they cannot omit it from their lives without a terrible loss being experienced. Burgess found that fathers who were most successful at work were those who had quality relationships with their children and that those relationships impacted positively on the father's own life, the children and the marital relationship.

So how much time do children need to spend with their father? As much as they do with their mother. The era of the father remaining aloof and distant from the family unit is fast receding, and the greater his involvement in children's lives and the life of the family, the better it is for everyone in that unit, practically and emotionally.

HOW MUCH TIME DO CHILDREN NEED AS PART OF THEIR FAMILY UNIT?

As our lives become increasingly manic and schedules take precedence over everything else, it becomes increasingly difficult for the family unit to function and come together. Children's schedules are now almost as hectic as those of their parents; the home serves as a base from which these busy schedules are launched. Parents pass each other in the doorway, collecting and delivering children to and from their organised activities. Weekend days are crammed with activities for both parents and children. An added complication is that children frequently do not attend schools in their areas and have to be delivered and collected from friend's houses. Due to the fact that there may be a number of children going in different directions, and because children go fewer and fewer places on their own, almost a full-time commuting system is required. But children need time with both parents together and with siblings. They need to see the parents together, co-operating, working, talking, having fun. It is a requisite of growing up that children get an experience of an adult intimate relationship working well, as so much of their learning and expectations about relationships and family life will come from this time. They need to see expressions of love and affection between their parents and feel themselves securely part of that. At holiday times, particularly Christmas, families are thrown together and if they don't have a familiarity with being together, tensions arise and tempers erupt. Time with siblings is significant also as children learn to experience themselves in terms of older and younger members of the household. Children learn how to be in groupings from their family experiences.

A family needs to have some time together every day, some time at weekends, and long holiday periods in order to retain a close intimate knowledge of each other.

DIVORCE AND SEPARATION

When a separation or divorce occurs there is a period of trauma and bereavement for the child. A mutually agreed, non-contentious break-up, where the couple can maintain boundaries between their own upset and loss and the child's needs, provides the easiest passage. Children studied long-term at the Judith Wallerstein Centre in California have indicated that a parental divorce is one of the most calamitous things to happen, and the effects are felt into middle age. 'Children become caught up in loyalty conflicts where they are forced to make unholy alliances with adults on either side of the battle in order to ensure that they continue to feel loved,' Jan Johnston, a director of that centre, has said. A possible outcome of the divorce is that one parent drops out of the child's life, activating a whole series of losses throughout the child's life. Where there is a third party involved, each parent may decide to give one side of the story to the children and thus involve them in unnecessary conflict. Parents can choose to end their own relationship, but from the day a child is born a life-long relationship with both his parents commences and he will endeavour to negotiate those relationships for the rest of his life.

Custody is granted to the mother in the majority of cases in Ireland, and the father-child relationship can be reduced to a relationship of phone calls and a few hours a week together. It amazes me how fathers who, until that separation, have been very active in the lives of their children, now accept only seeing them at weekends and perhaps one evening in the week. It is not surprising that children often feel confused, bewildered and abandoned, caught in the conflictual and conflicting emotions of their parents. It is heart-wrenching to be separated from your children, and many separated fathers feel overwhelmed by that loss but fail to deal with it. They resort to defensive behaviour, cutting off emotionally and distancing themselves from their children. The children feel rejected and forsaken, made to suffer for something not of their choosing. They need to be reassured constantly by both parents of their love and commitment to them, and to experience that care being put into operation. So often people offer rhetoric to their children, but what the children read are the actions of the parents, which may be in direct contrast to the verbal statement.

During this traumatic period the children may become difficult, unco-operative, truculent and angry and express the desire not to see the parent who has left the family home. Routines need to be held on to; changes can be discussed later. It is important for both parents to agree that contact with both parents must be maintained (provided, of course, that no type of abuse has occurred) regardless of expressions of lack of interest. Parents need to remain parents and consider what is best for the child, not what would fuel vengeful fantasies. Co-operation is necessary and if the separating couple cannot furnish that, they must seek assistance in order to bring it about. Questions of allegiance, who is to blame for the break-up and which parent is more capable and responsible ought never to be entered into. The children are suffering and need support and care to see them through. Occasionally siblings may choose to live with different parents; the sibling relationship must be nurtured; they need to spend time together and affiliations should not be allowed to damage their relationship.

Where possible, parents should endeavour to come together for events in the child's life, not just major events like Christmas or weddings. In a recent interview, the actor Gabriel Byrne said in response to a query about his amiable relationship with his ex-wife Ellen Barkin, 'I've always worked hard towards that because to me, if you've been intimate with somebody emotionally, I think you form a bond with that person. And when you have kids you're connected even more closely. Ellen is the mother of my kids and I'm their father, so we're always going to be connected and it makes absolute sense that we should be as respectful and friendly as we possibly can.' I've seen children extremely anxious about how the separated couple are going to get along at such events; this ought not to be their concern. Children need to see adults managing conflicts and difficulties. This is partly how they learn emotional literacy. If parents have not learned themselves how to be emotionally literate during their relationship and deal well with conflictual situations, it is now utterly imperative that they do. Their problems may be solved simply because they are getting rid of each other out of their lives, but their children will continually be obliged to deal with their relationship. Parents have a responsibility, when unhappy and wishing to end a relationship, not to just do so by falling in love with someone else. This makes the ending harder for everyone to negotiate and is really reneging not only on your responsibility to know what's happening for you (emotional literacy) but also to address and deal with it before involving a third party.

STEP-PARENTS AND STEP-SIBLINGS

This is the era of change and mobility; family groupings may change more than once in a childhood. Children become accustomed to step-siblings whom they are subsequently separated from. Where there is not a blood relationship, the impact and loss of that relationship may go unnoticed amidst a lot of other variables. Children must adapt and go on with their lives, and because they are resilient and resourceful they may seem to be taking it all in their stride. As parents, we then reassure ourselves that all is well, and unless the children display some behavioural or psychological difficulty that is where things are left. Wouldn't it be better to err on the side of assuming some difficulties? Then if children genuinely seem to be handling the changes well, so much the better?

Children may change their family grouping, home, school, location and, having done that once, may be required to do so a second time. The success rate of second relationships tends to be no higher than the first. Children can be required to deal with aspects of the break-up that a spouse can't face – like a new partner or the existence of a half-sibling. Too much is asked of children in break-ups and sometimes too little is asked of the separating couple. Stability and predictability have a part to play in a child's security, and disrupting those, without it being absolutely necessary, is foolhardy. Obviously there are relationships where it is clearly better for everyone involved, including the children, that it ends, but also there are circumstances and situations where if professional help was sought, accepted, and a process of change entertained, matters could be resolved. Frequently by the time a couple considers such assistance, the marriage is already disintegrating and little can be done to retrieve matters. Often the difficulties are denied until another partner is found, then either a pattern of long-term deception is set in motion or decisions are rushed, backed by ultimatums. Couples need as much assistance to end a relationship as to recommit to it; seeking professional help can make either decision more tenable.

Chapter 5

FEMINIST PERSPECTIVES

The traditional idea of family has drastically changed. There are single-parent families, merged families, gay parent families where children have two mothers and no father or two fathers and no mother, families where one parent has changed sex, families where former heterosexual parents now understand their sexual orientation to be homosexual and are currently engaged in a homosexual liaison. Individuals and gay couples succeed in adopting babies. Surrogacy is utilised more and more frequently. The conceptualisation of families and parents is being stretched to the limits. The situation in Ireland is no different.

The structure of families is becoming transient and impermanent. This, naturally, causes an insecurity and sometimes encourages a regression to a previous state or set of values. In the United States, such evangelical reversals have gained in popularity; calls for a return to family values, or 'the traditional family', have been vocal and this movement, termed 'the new familism', has a certain following. A new men's movement called the 'Promise Keepers' wishes to reassert men's traditional role as head of the family and has held mass demonstrations putting forward those views. Such reversals have a rigid focus and have few merits. Gains exist, for sure, in terms of security where roles are rigid and inflexible and everyone knows what is expected of them. Such gains may be material or financial as, instead of couples grappling with schedules, childminding, shopping and so on, roles are set, but it is not the way forward, it is a retreat into fear. Men are feeling threatened because their traditional role of head of the family is being eroded, but there is so much more to be gained if they can step forward into the intimacy of the family and leave that cold, isolated position of 'head'. Attempting to claw that back is only going to leave them more and more deficient in the actual skills of parenting and partnership which are required for the future.

The general thrust in relationships now tends to be towards intimacy. Today's couples want real, companionable relationships with each other. Individuals will choose to live on a meagre income or change their material circumstances for personal autonomy and happiness; they feel material wealth can be regained later. Making huge compromises to facilitate one aspect of your life is no longer seen as a healthy way to operate.

I suggest that the 'provider role' is slowly becoming dysfunctional. It is no longer a viable way for couples to live if marriages are to be psychologically 'growthful' vehicles moving towards self-realisation and autonomy. In a piece of research carried out by Blumstein and Schwartz, the power of decision-making within the couple was seen to correlate with income. This is not to suggest that one person, male or female, taking the role of provider for a specific number of years is inoperable. It can prove to be a successful way of taking care of the childcare dilemma and/or offering opportunities for further study, or pursuing a new career which isn't going to be financially viable immediately. It's important to remember that it will work if a) it's for an agreed length of time and b) if the other partner can also avail of this opportunity if he/she so desires. The problem lies in the long-term nature of the 'provider role' – the 'signed up for life' certainty of it.

Another piece of research showed how economic dependency can cause dishonesty. Many female, financially dependent spouses maintained some kind of 'hidden money' – secret bank accounts, dishonesty regarding cost purchases, purchases undisclosed and so on. Likewise, I've known many women who used shopping as a method of punishing their husbands for some untold deed, or who expected that their husbands would clear overdrafts and credit cards without a grumble.

Equally I've known manipulating husbands who withheld amounts from communal finance for their own private excursions when there wasn't really a surplus. Duplicity and outwitting each other can become part of the partnership when financial parity does not exist. It's probably necessary, for all couples, whatever the source of their financial income, to have communal finances, used for the family's needs, but with some money, however little, kept separate for each person's individual needs.

So is the lot of men difficult? I, as a woman, think that women have had a rotten time but I feel men have had an equally vile history. They can be expected to maintain spouses, children and ex-spouses for their lifetimes and in today's climate, get very little gratitude for it. I noted my own surprise recently when a woman, speaking to me about her concern for her husband and his choices in life, said, 'Well, he's financially maintained myself and the children through their childhood and that's no mean feat'. Men die earlier, suffer more health problems and are at much greater risk of committing suicide, murder or other violent crimes and of living out isolated, lonely lives. Most women I speak to would not like to have the sole financial responsibility for their family.

Children need their fathers in a constant, interactive manner. They need fathers who inform themselves about their children's outer and inner lives. Very often it is the mother who has her finger on the pulse of the family, noting who seems to be upset or not coping. Fathers now need to enter that realm, not only to be available to their children when there's some crisis but in a daily manner, for the small occurrences in a child's life as well as the major events. Men are used to having their lives upheld and supported by their partners. Now they are being asked to move from that position and be available to uphold their children's lives. Two is better than one and children will benefit greatly from this input from both parents. For their own sakes as well as their children, fathers, though many may not yet know it, need constant, regular intimate contact with their children. But this cannot be achieved if men continue to work 50 hours a week. The mother must take joint financial responsibility. There is no point in women continuing to demand that fathers spend more time with their children when they are not being given the responsibility for doing that. Sometimes couples say, 'But we're happy in this way, we are in fact equal. He brings in the money and I do the vast majority of childcare.' But what about the children? They grow up over-bonded to the mother and with a father who gets close to them during holiday periods and then withdraws again.

The old syndrome still exists: 'Don't tell your father.' Adult children can have abortions, encounter difficulties in their love relations, face feelings of failure in courses or jobs, make plans for emigration, solely with the support of one parent, the mother. Fathers are still protected from the dramas of family life and are therefore shut out from that inner world. Sometimes they can't be told because of concern about their likely reactions; in other words, either the mother or child would have to spend time comforting or appeasing the father. Instead of the child getting the assistance required, the parent would take centre stage. Sometimes decisions are made or the drama dealt with before the father hears about it. Of course, this is insulting to the father, but how many fathers object and ask for things to be done differently? Some relish their protection and are loath to give it up. In psychoanalytical jargon, the female psyche offers containment (structure and nurturance) to the life of the family. It is time for the male psyche to extend beyond the world of the self to his children, and to truly assist them in equipping themselves to live life fully and healthily.

The 'fairness perspective' must be used now to argue the case for men being entitled to inclusion in their children's lives. Women are entitled to work outside the home, experience the benefits of that and not be overburdened with domestic chores. Men are entitled not to have to carry the financial burden of the family and to have more time with their children. The traditional role of 'provider' does not allow for either of these positions. Lamb et al (1987) found that in two-parent families where the mother is not employed outside the home, fathers spend 20-25 per cent of the time that mothers spend in direct engagement with the children. Where the mother worked outside the home the level rose to 33 per cent. One would expect a much greater increase if the childcare was truly being shared, but as we know working mothers continue to perform the majority of childcare tasks even when working full-time.

Of course many tasks will be performed by neither parent but rather the childminder. The children have needs and rights within this scenario. It isn't just about what women want and what men desire, there is a third party whose consideration must remain part of the central focus. Most adults I speak to wish that they'd had more contact with their father while growing up; unfortunately, the vast majority then go on to replicate that scenario with their own children. Working long hours is not the only reason men don't spend time with their children, but at least changing that can perhaps move things along more fairly. Raising children must become a joint responsibility. It is a serious business and something that other countries take more seriously than we do. My own experience of childcare is that it cannot remain in the chore category. It is appropriate that you'd want to spend time with your children; if you don't feel that need or desire, then it's important to face that and understand more about it. You've had this child, now why will you not take a primary responsibility in raising her? Often, just like men reporting on their involvement with their children, adult children carry illusions about their father's involvement with them. Closer examination frequently reveals a different picture. Adult children usually have plenty to say about their mothers; in other words they can illustrate that they know the person well. This is not the case with fathers. When people in groups are asked to speak about their fathers, they have much less to say about the person and a great deal about the loss or lack of a relationship with him.

Young men in their teens and early twenties are showing great potential, I feel. They are capable of articulating their inner emotions, and seek wider options in terms of relationships and life than their fathers. Will they be able to continue to nourish those aspects when they enter the world of work and responsibility? Since they are frequently without role models, it may prove difficult.

While many men have supported feminism, there has also been an insidious backlash through the 1980s and 1990s as outlined by Susan Faludi in *Backlash*. She shows that men have not been idle and that women have no reason whatsoever to feel complacent about the gains through feminism. She describes the road ahead and the amount of progress still to be made but more importantly she names the undercurrent existing, right across occupations, which seeks to drag back the energetic thrust forward of women and equality. She quotes collusion after collusion with this backlash right across the media and the professions, and claims that the environment and areas which women have entered have proven to be harsh and unyielding. Women, because they are accustomed to things being difficult for them, hardly notice. 'Each woman in her own way persisted in pushing against it. This quiet female resistance was the uncelebrated counterpoint to the anti-feminist campaign of the 1980s, a common thread in the narrative of so many women's lives, no matter where they belonged on the ideological spectrum, no matter what their rung on the class ladder.'

Many people are concerned that if women take joint financial responsibility long-term for their families (and I'm saying this must occur if we are to have equal and peer relationships between men and women), the maternal tradition, which has been so lauded, will be lost. In my opinion, the valuable things within that tradition such as a deep-rooted connectedness to the source of life and an openness to emotions and intuition, will survive the transition, and indeed only be enhanced, by women not having to make territorial-type choices. The problem has been, and continues to be, when women try to be in the world of work as men have been, and suppress their emotions in order to walk the male treadmill of success. We've had well-known examples of women who've achieved success by these means and become steely ice as a result. The route to freedom for women or men is not in suppressing feelings and conflicts but in listening to them and sometimes voicing them. Indicating how difficult it is to change that environment and bring female values to bear on it, Jayne Buxton says in *Ending the Mother War*, 'The truth is that all the family-friendly policies in the western world added together do not yet amount to more than a pin-prick on the surface of that immovable, sluggish giant – the family-ignorant workplace culture'. Susie Orbach, in her book *What's Really Going On Here* says that we must move towards an emotional literacy in public and private lives if we are to live decent, moral, integrated lives: 'What we are wanting and seeking in our relationships both private and public is recognition, emotional connection and a chance to understand and express the deepest parts of our own self.'

Equally, a whole new male tradition of paternity can bring males a more integrated, holistic, nurturing life. The 'new man' much maligned, criticised and disparagingly represented throughout the 1990s, only seen to be taking on changes in response to the feminist movement and emulating values not seen as male, could finally achieve respect. Many male writers, Robert Bly being the best known, have tried to counter this, but not very successfully. Throughout the 1980s and 1990s Bly attempted to encourage men to reconnect with a sense of male-ness through all-male workshops and weekends in the forests. He spoke of the soft male, and recovering the wild man within. In a newly-published book called *Stiffed, the betrayal of the modern man*, Susan Faludi speaks of men being in crisis. She sees their crisis as stemming from cultural, economic and political matters rather than the fact that women are gaining equality. Women, she states, had one major advantage when the feminist movement began – they could identify men and the trappings of patriarchy as the enemy and were motivated to act. Men are fighting intan-gible enemies. 'In an attempt to employ the old paradigm, men have invented antagonists to make their problems visible, but with the passage of time, the culprits – scheming feminists, affirmative-action proponents, job-grabbing illegal aliens, the wife of a president – have come to seem increasingly unconvincing as explanations for their situation. Defeating such paper tigers offers no sense of victory.' She advocates that men move out further to champion a revolution where there is no enemy – 'create a new paradigm' and help create a freer, more humane world for everyone. Anthony Clare, in *On Men: Masculinity in Crisis*, clearly outlines the male dilemma: 'Phallic man, authoritative, dominant, assertive – man in control not merely of himself but of woman – is starting to die, and now the question is whether a man will emerge phoenix-like in his place or whether man himself will become largely redundant.'

Perhaps the essential question is, as Diane Ehrensaft puts it, 'Are these ideas of men and women revolutionary or evolutionary?' Both perhaps, but it does seem that the ideas of peer relationship and co-parenting are the psychologically healthy option for everyone. The suggestion that the only work women must devote themselves to is taking care of their children and partner is a myth, part of no one's tradition. As Penelope Leach says, 'Full time, exclusive motherhood is often assumed to be an integral part of women's traditional role. The idea that women should do no work other than care for children (and that the most privileged, who did not do their own caring, should do no work) is not part of anybody's tradition, having a short history and a political provenance.' Women have been duped into believing that if they are not with their children all of their waking hours, then they are letting down the maternal tradition. Within the feminist movement of the 1960s and 1970s, marriage and motherhood were seen as something for women to escape from, not to be valued. Feminists who married and had children were seen as letting down the side, and buying the 'lie' that you could be happy with a man. This old brand of feminism is still stoically put forward by Germaine Greer, though another avid feminist, Gloria Steinham, recently married for the first time at the age of 66! Thus, a dichotomy was created and continues to exist between motherhood and its associated values, and wanting equality in the workplace and life in general.

In *The New Feminism*, Natasha Walter asks whether feminism still has a role to play. She comes down very strongly with the opinion that while much has changed for women, still a lot remains unchanged. She says, 'the constraints that operate upon women are still fierce' and as evidence she quotes the facts that 93 per cent of university professors are men, 96 per cent of surgeons are men and 96 per cent of company directors are men. She says that the 'new feminism' is materialistic; 'It concentrates on the material reality of inequality and allows women to live their personal lives without the constraints of a rigid ideology.' I feel feminism has helped to achieve a great deal for women and will continue to illuminate thoughts on inequality. There is still a lot to be changed and it will change, in time. 'Feminism in the twentieth century has already achieved half a revolution. Now as we approach the twenty-first century, it is time to look to the next half,' says Natasha Walter.

So perhaps these are evolutionary times and men and women, attempting to respond to a multitudinous sea of emotions, needs and attempts at self-actualisation, are struggling courageously to find a way in which couples can come together and care for their offspring. One hunter-gatherer tribe, the Curripaco, who live in the tropical rainforest of north-west Amazonia, practice a concept called 'partible paternity' which states that every man who contributes sperm during a pregnancy contributes to the biological existence of the child. The practice has many advantages: children with multiple fathers are more likely to survive as the secondary fathers take a responsibility for the child also and the ranking of main father and secondary fathers is agreed between all the participants and determined by who had more sexual access to the woman. This sort of research raises questions, according to Dr Stephen Beckerman, Associate Professor of Anthropology at Pennsylvania State University, about the supposed evolutionary

bargain between men and women. 'The bargain, that men sup-
ply the resources in return for female fidelity and guaranteed
paternity, may not exist.' Robin Baker, author of *Sperm Wars* has
said that while partible paternity as a concept doesn't exist for
us in the western world, our behaviour matches it! His research
has shown that ten per cent of children born within marriage in
Britain were not the children of the husband.

In the majority of cases, men seem to be the movable factor
when marriages break up. Generally the children remain with
the mother and if she forms another relationship, that man will
move in with them in a parental role. Time and time again I see
men with say, for example, three children, moving in with a
divorced woman with three children, whom they now will be
helping to bring up. A lot of men are helping to raise children
who aren't theirs, while their own children are living with other
surrogate fathers. This will create even more distance between
fathers and their children. They will always be in a secondary or
outside position with their step-children and yet may be spending an insufficient amount of time with their own children to
maintain a close, intense relationship with them.

HOW MUCH TIME DO PARENTS NEED TO HAVE WITH THEIR CHILDREN?

Down through the years there's been a lot of talk about maternal
instinct, and sometimes the assumption is made that a woman
bonds easily and naturally with her baby but that the man may
have to work at it. If a woman doesn't experience a well of emotion immediately, she will very often feel that she's wrong and
will prove to be a 'bad mother'. But everyone is different. The
ideal is, of course, where a child is joyfully received but after a
difficult and frightening labour, the mother may be wondering
what she's let herself in for and the father may be in shock.
While it is wonderful if the relationship is immediate, it may
take time for both the mother and father to enter a strong life-
enduring relationship with the child. The child is vulnerable,
needy and demanding and that may be frightening to adults

who feel they keep their own urgent needs under lock and key. But the child is also wonderful in his/her vulnerability, and parents can be awed into a relationship if they will only succumb to it! Hence the need for a long, uninterrupted, unhurried time with the baby. This is a crucial time in the building of the relationship with the child and it will never come again, so it must be prioritised. If the parents are emotionally experiencing a lot of difficulty (the birth of a child can churn up a lot of unresolved emotions as well as evoke new ones), then it's imperative that support is sought, ideally from relatives who will also be building enduring relationships with the baby. The parents need time to adjust to the inclusion of this baby within their coupleship or family, and that means spending time together, not just individual time, with the baby. The baby will feel that communal joy or welcome and be warmed by it.

HOW MUCH TIME DO PARENTS NEED TO REINFORCE THAT BOND?

It is not a question of 'absence makes the heart grow fonder' when dealing with the parental relationship to children. It may be alluring to carry a child's photo or drawing with you while away from him, but it is important to remember that the enduring safeguard, ensuring that you will remain open to your child, will be to develop and retain a strong emotional connection to him. This is facilitated predominantly by spending time with him. I'm not saying that spending time with a child will guarantee an emotional connection, but time will serve as a context within which, if one is open and communicative, such bonding can continue to be renewed. This is frequently borne out by divorced or separated fathers who feel that their once-a-week contact with the child is insufficient.

As a parent, sometimes all the energy and focus will go on what the child needs but it is important to remember that parenting and this life-long connection with a child has a lot to offer you as a parent. It is a durable love connection, inspiring in its freshness. It offers you a possibility of reconnecting with your own childhood emotions and joys and seeing things differently, responding spontaneously and creatively and simply having fun. Enjoying and admiring a child is probably the most loving thing you can offer, not in the sense of the child being an extension of you but as himself, separate, complete and wondrous. Parents frequently forget how much they can learn from their offspring in terms of new perspectives forged through responding to their inquiries about the world.

HOW MUCH TIME CAN PARENTS TOLERATE WITH THEIR CHILDREN?

Now, this is perhaps the million-dollar question! Judging from the amount of time children spend in crèches, school, after-school activities, participating in organised hobbies, and attending extra-curricular classes, it seems that parents can't tolerate much time with their offspring. We know that children need time with parents and that parents need time with children, so what is all this 'busyness' about? Of course, it may be ill-informed parenting, but is it symptomatic of difficulties in the parent-child relationship? Our society continues to talk of the value of communication and valuing interpersonal skills, but is this a case of rhetoric while at the same time we move further and further away from the essentials within that concept? Parenting is difficult, everyone agrees; being with children and responding to their needs and demands is exacting. It is burdensome to feel that you are not doing very well, or achieving much or being very appreciated. But this era is shackled with the responsibility of knowledge and consciousness; we cannot plead ignorance. We know when we are not doing a good job, but to investigate why we are not parenting as well as we'd like to, or might be capable of, means entering a terrain of complex emotions and values where your own sentiments merge and conflict with your child's. Child rearing may rekindle memories from our own childhoods we wanted to forget. Parents feel their inadequacy and vulnerability in the face of their child's tenacity, rage or stubbornness. Messy, incomprehensible and awkward emotions are evoked. Sometimes one's sense of competence, effectiveness and ability to think rationally is seriously undermined. I've seen parents who, in high profile jobs, are the epitome of proficiency and conciliation, reduced to blubbering tears or incomprehensible mutterings after 30 minutes doing battle with a pugnacious three-year-old!

While the topic of this book is children, and how we are caring for them, I'm constantly aware of how much is being demanded of parents, and how the parameter is relentlessly widening. It requires confidence to know when one needs help, and too often things are left muddling along until some behavioural or psychological symptom manifests with the child. Parents need assistance to do the job well; that help may simply be a conversation with a friend or colleague. Communication is important, and not just the banter that parents often engage in about their offspring. I recall one work situation where, in our break-times, we had intriguing conversations about childcare even though the majority of us were not parents. Those who were parents would often pose dilemmas which we would all then offer ideas and opinions about. The parent usually went away from the discussion better informed and, at the least, unburdened.

WHEN THE MOTHER'S SOLE CAREER IS CHILD REARING, WHAT HAPPENS WHEN THE CHILDREN LEAVE?

Only 26 years ago, the 'marriage bar' obliged women to retire on marriage from a variety of jobs in the public service. This was removed in 1973. Women who have decided to work in the home full-time have done so for a number of reasons.

1.) They understood, prior to marriage, that that was how they'd like things to be, and entered into the marriage on the assumption that their partner would be the breadwinner for the entirety of their relationship, or the rest of their lives if they divorced or separated. I've met men who, though financially maintaining a second partner and children, were obliged also to financially maintain the first wife (as they understood, forever) even though she had been allocated the family home. Equally, I've met the second partners in similar situations, where the second wife feels aggrieved because part of her income is contributing towards the first partner, who chooses not to work outside the home. Regarding the financial maintenance of children, I don't think anyone disagrees that that must be honoured, or that a divorced wife, who up to then has been a homemaker with the agreement of both parties, must be facilitated financially over an agreed length of time until she finds a new career or retrains.

2.) Those who see housewifery and child rearing as more emotionally rewarding, stimulating and satisfying than the paid employment available to them. Some jobs are not very interesting and are done purely for the financial gain. When I was in my early twenties, I taught in an all-girls' working-class secondary school where I made my views on women and women's rights clearly known. One day, while I was pontificating about the value for women of paid employment, having their financial independence and so on, I was called to task by one bright young student who explained that the only kind of work any of their mothers were trained to do was boring and badly paid. Weren't they much better off at home caring for their children when they had husbands who would do such work? Fairness didn't come into it for her; their fathers were willing to do it, so let them.

3.) Those who would have to face spousal opposition to work outside the home. This grouping is diminishing, but as a child and teenager I heard frequent references to men not *allowing* women to pursue their careers after marriage: 'I wouldn't have my wife working' or 'my husband wouldn't want me to work.' Lack of co-operation can take many forms and can ultimately wear someone down. A great many women who work full-time outside the home experience this, but not to a degree which prevents them from continuing working. Nor is it maliciously done; it is simply that men find it harder to 'see' the things that have to be done to facilitate the running of a home, or to think about the

93

things that need to be sorted or wondered about.

4.) Lack of satisfactory childminding arrangements prevents many women from remaining in employment. These include women who tried to continue to work after the birth of a child but capitulated in the face of scant support and unsatisfactory services. Such people usually experience an incredible loss in not being able to pursue their careers but can't see a solution. If there isn't a financial need for that spouse to work, then she may receive little sympathy or support from friends or colleagues. I've seen mothers of three or four children who have struggled for years to continue their professional work, but eventually stay home full-time because they are exhausted from doing two jobs, having a partner who wasn't doing his half. Such women retire quietly from their professions and may never take them up again. The system, i.e., the family, may function much better, but the workforce has lost a valuable contributor, with years of experience. Within most professions and jobs new techniques and methods emerge all the time, and it can become intimidating after a few years out to return to work.

5.) Women lose confidence in their abilities when they are away from work for a number of years. They may have grown away from the previous work, but cannot consider what other work they might wish to engage in. FÁS 'return to work' courses are excellent for building confidence and offering new possibilities. Running a home and taking care of children require a huge variety of skills, and women sometimes forget that. Being multi-focused, dealing with arguments, managing finances and time, being quick-thinking, overseeing all kinds of tasks, 'keeping your head when all about you are losing theirs and blaming it on you', are only a few of the skills developed in home-making. Employers are beginning to realise this and in some areas of employment there are opportunities for women in their fifties and sixties whom employers see as reliable, hardworking, innovative and self-reliant.

6.) Penal tax and welfare systems discourage women from remaining in employment or returning to it. A huge percentage of earnings is paid in taxation and, combined with high child-minding fees, it may not seem financially worthwhile for both partners to work. Speaking to a number of women who had families and returned to employment in their mid-forties, it became clear that the extra outlays easily gobbled up the amount of salary they were left with after tax. People listed childminding and babysitting costs, convenience meals, extra car and house cleaning as costs that would not otherwise have been incurred. It's interesting to note that all of these payments had to be made out of the female salary, which then gave an ever-diminishing experience of financial earning. If she decided to revert to not working, all of these expenses would disappear. However, all of the women I spoke to loved their jobs and had no intention of giving them up.

So, what happens when the mother's work is done and only a partner remains to be taken care of? Is it reasonable to take care of another physically healthy adult who is, or ought to be, fully capable of taking care of himself? I've frequently heard men in their fifties and sixties, on becoming divorced or widowed, proclaim quite proudly their inability to cook, shop or iron clothes. A cleaner or housekeeper is brought in or laundry services are used. Such men have moved from mother to wife and never learned one of the most essential life skills, to simply care for yourself. Frequently, such men find another wife soon. Women, on the other hand, may never learn fully the skill of fending for themselves.

So what do women do with their time and energy when the task of childrearing is complete? The two areas which probably absorb most of this vitality are hobbies and charity work, essentially a life of retirement. I've spoken to such women and posed the question: what happens if your breadwinner partner decides to leave you? The response has been that he will have to continue to offer financial support. To the question of 'what happens if you want to leave?' the response was that the new partner would have to be in a position to financially support them. Is this a healthy response for adult women to give?

Chapter 6

THE AGE OF ANXIETY

This is the age of anxiety. The rapidity of change, particularly in the technological area, means that we are racing ahead of ourselves. The whole notion of progress is a complex one and there are those who would argue that we are losing touch entirely with our past and therefore will not be able to utilise it as a resource to learn from. According to Richard Bronk in *Progress and the Invisible Hand*, some social historians state that the past is dying as a relevant factor in contemporary life. 'The young, too, living exclusively in the present may have no touchstone against which to value the new,' he says. Emotional illiteracy is commonly named as the difficulty and such behaviours as violence, suicide, rape, and psychological disturbances such as eating disorders and mental illness are manifestations of this. In Ireland one person commits suicide every day and a quarter of those are aged under 24. Eating disorders are on the increase, with a prominent percentage of teenage girls suffering from anorexia or bulimia. Ireland's first day-care centre for homeless young people, 'The Loft', opened in November 1999. While it seeks to provide shelter and meals, it aims to keep the teenagers off the streets during the day and offer links back into education and other programmes. Focus Ireland say that about twenty per cent of the people who use their service are under fourteen years of age.

Parents are not managing or keeping charge of their children. The style of parenting has changed greatly over the last fifteen to twenty years and parents don't know how to cope.

Young people are articulate and can appear more confident or capable than they actually are. They are being given rights and responsibilities beyond their abilities. Parents must remain in a guiding role. Often it seems that parents, particularly those who've become parents at a young age, wish to encourage a sibling relationship with their teenage children. This is not a peership, it is a parent-child relationship, and parents must show that they have the ability to parent even in difficult and trying circumstances. Sharing intimacies about your own love-life or conflicts is usually not advisable; it is better to leave that space for your children to explain their difficulties. Parents are afraid of incurring their teenagers' disapproval and will often compromise their own values because they are told that 'a friend is allowed' to do the activity under discussion.

Frequently, teenagers say that their parents have no idea what they get up to in their recreational time. Parents are frightened and wish to remain oblivious to the specifics of their teenagers' entertainment, but these teenagers do need parental supervision. Check in detail where they are going and who with, check out venues and activities. Keep aware and up-to-date on their friendships. If they are staying overnight check:

a) that there are parents there and

b) that they are actually staying where they say.

Other parents may have different standards. Be reasonable and open to discussion but also continue to hold an awareness of your own values and those which you wish to encourage in your teenagers.

Our children are becoming more 'unwell' in every sense of that word. Stephen Covey in *The Seven Habits of Highly Effective Families* speaks of how the major problems encountered by teachers in American high schools have changed over the past 50 years. In 1940, the offences were chewing gum or speaking out of turn, now they are rape, assault, drug abuse, teenage pregnancy and so on. This is serious: teenagers and children today are killing themselves, committing acts of violence against themselves and others, and drugging themselves out of consciousness. Also occurring are problems in school, difficulties in learning, phobic and anxiety reactions and, most troubling, eating disorders. The most common nutritional disorder in the developed world is obesity.

In his book *Emotional Intelligence*, Goleman speaks of the seriousness of the problem and utilises research from a national sample of American children aged seven to sixteen years, comparing their emotional condition in the mid 1970s and at the end of the 1980s, to support his argument. There was a steady decrease in ability to cope. Based on parents' and teachers' assessments more children were doing poorly. More children were withdrawn or encountering social problems, more children were experiencing symptoms of anxiety and depression, more children were having problems with keeping their attention or being focused, and delinquent and aggressive tendencies had increased.

In the United States, the National Institute of Mental Health announced in the early 1990s that twenty per cent of children need psychiatric care. This is a staggering statistic, naturally begging the question why? Peter Breggin, who wrote *Toxic Psychiatry*, believes that the response of society to label and drug children whose behaviour is aberrant is too easily entertained. Like R.D. Laing before him, he suggests that a much fuller explanation of the context often reveals the sanity of the response. Children are in a way sacrificed because neither parents nor authorities will face what the child and his/her symptoms are naming. I have never met a child who, after I spoke with him, baffled me. When children or teenagers are able to speak about their lives and difficulties, whatever the circumstance and however bizarre their script or motivating force, their lives usually become comprehensible in the context of their biographical data. But who wants to listen? Who has the time to commit to these children, in order to understand their problems, and who is willing to be available to steer them through their pain? The 'chemical imbalance' argument means that everyone is absolved from blame. There is nothing to be done except follow the prescribed course of medication. Breggin calls it suppressing the passion of children; I would call it suppressing the soul of children. We are losing sight of our real selves and wandering aimlessly without any clear concept of what life means to us. Benjamin Spock says, 'We have lost much of our sense of dignity as individuals, we don't have souls anymore'. Once again, our children are paying the price; ill-equipped and bungling their way through childhood and adolescence, they display prodigious symptoms of distress which frequently lead to tragic consequences.

So the child enters the world of prescribed medication. Many people involved in childcare are appalled at the increasing number of children taking prescribed medication for some form of mental illness. In the United States the number of children taking prescribed medication increases each year. Peter Breggin has tabulated the effects of such medication, and suggests that the side-effects in many cases do not justify the usage. The price is enormous for the child. I've worked with many survivors of our mental health care system, people who hated being on medication because of how it affected their thinking and emotional responses, and yet were given no assistance to come off that medication. Many came off without the help of a medical practitioner, which can be dangerous. Yet drug companies, making billions, continue to advertise such products and suppress information regarding the side-effects.

When are we going to understand and appreciate the value of difficulties? We constantly validate the child who fits in, causes no trouble and seeks nothing extraordinary; anything outside of this fairly narrow band is seen as troublesome and worthy of a negative response. If, as mature adults, we could interpret the child's problem or behaviour as a plea for assistance, or greater communication at the very least, we might serve the child, ourselves and society so much better. Difficulties arise because something is amiss in that situation. If we could keep things simple and respond from our hearts to the soul of the child in trouble, I suggest we might actually be of some assistance. Instead, we keep our distance, diagnose and medicate, and ultimately succeed in silencing the child and burying the problem, thereby discouraging him from finding resources within himself which would assist him in similar difficulties later. It would take a major shift in perspective, a paradigm shift, to see difficulties as an opportunity – the translation of crisis in Chinese is 'critical opportunity'. Suppose we were to see the crises which children and teenagers present us with as just such an opportunity, a serious possibility – filled opportunity. How often do we hear the phrase, 'he/she never gave an ounce of trouble so I don't understand how this happened' in response to something awful that has occurred in late teens/early twenties. Goleman says in *Emotional Intelligence*, 'A new kind of toxicity is sweeping into and poisoning the very experience of childhood, signifying sweeping deficits in emotional competences'. Our children and teenagers do not have the resources to deal with what life presents them with, and in the 'assistance' offered to them further damage is often done.

Thomas Moore in *Care of the Soul*, sees symptoms as pertaining to the soul of the person, an expression which ought not simply be eradicated. He talks of engagement, deep caring and the path of the soul as a way of understanding such symptoms and their relevance in that particular person's life. He displays a reverence for the symptoms as much as the person, and feels that effective help is not simply about a cure but much more about understanding that person's journey through life towards the self.

But mental illness is not the only reason for administering medication. Children who are deemed to be hyperactive or suffering from ADD (attention deficit disorder) frequently receive prescribed medication. ADD is characterised by overactivity, restlessness, inattention and failure to persist with given tasks. Very often it is said to manifest in the first five years but can occur later and occurs more frequently in boys. Essentially it is an excess of energy and a demand for attention. With medication, children become more subdued and more focused and obviously less difficult. Hyperactive children are difficult to deal with within a school environment and because our educational system isn't geared towards difference, it becomes necessary to find a way for such children to 'fit in'. The medical argument is that there is a biochemical imbalance in the brain which needs to be redressed.

Young people are self-medicating with drugs, alcohol and smoking but it can be strongly argued they are merely imitating the behaviour of their adult mentors. The cost in our society of alcohol-related illness, accidents, violence, sexual assault and absenteeism from work is enormous. We are an addicted society. Alcohol has created lives of hardship for many families; our history is steeped in alcoholism. By the age of sixteen, the majority of teenagers drink and if they haven't experimented with drugs, will be likely to do so by the age of twenty. According to a report issued in November 1999 by the European Monitoring Centre for Drugs and Drug Addiction, four out of every ten Irish sixteen-year-olds have tried cannabis and more than two per cent of the same age group have tried heroin. The majority of 6,000-7,000 drug-related deaths occurring in the EU each year are from heroin overdoses. In a 'Prime Time' report on RTE 1 in November 1999, research with fourteen to fifteen year olds indicated that over 80 per cent drank alcohol and 38 per cent had tried cannabis. The Rutland Addiction Centre has also seen an increase in the number of young people between the ages of seventeen to 25 years presenting for treatment.

In the United States alcohol-related accidents are the leading cause of death among people between fifteen and 24. Often young people drink to alleviate anxiety or shyness and find that they can be a different person when drunk. Inhibitions are discarded and a new freedom is found. Regarding sexual activity among fourteen to fifteen year-olds, the 'Prime Time' research found that 70 per cent were sexually active, usually in combination with drink. 32 per cent of boys and 28 per cent of girls had experienced oral sex while eighteen per cent of boys and eleven per cent of girls had had intercourse. Unfortunately, high consumption of alcohol brings with it other risks also. In America 90 per cent of all rapes reported on college campuses happened when either the victim or the perpetrator or both had been drinking. In Ireland a boy of seventeen was accused of rape by a fifteen-year-old in July 1999. What emerged was a story of drink and inappropriate sexual behaviour which occurred regularly between a group of teenagers. Unfortunately on a particular night this all ended in the circumstance before the court, where a young girl understood she had been raped. The boy was acquitted. The risks of over-drinking and drugging are enormous and not simply from the intake of the substances but from the physical and psychological hurt and damage which can be brought about because of the context. A context of being 'out of it', out of control, is sought and created. However, when things go too far someone is always made to pay. The context has been created whereby specific behaviour becomes acceptable, but if it runs too far out of control, one individual may still be seen as responsible.

Sexually transmitted diseases are on the increase among young people. Sufficient precautions are not being taken while sexual activity is engaged in. According to Dr Emer McHale, senior area medical officer with the Western Health Board and that region's AIDS co-ordinator, there has been an enormous increase in recent years in sexually transmitted infections among people under twenty. Figures from the Department of Health show that there were 32 new cases of AIDS in the first seven months of 1999 and 22 of those were children. In 1998 there were 136 cases. The Dublin AIDS Alliance believes that increasing confidence and self-esteem would help to combat the problem since if people care more for themselves, they will insist on their own health being protected.

Suicide, particularly among young males between the ages of fifteen and 24, is now the second most common cause of death in this country. According to Dr Kathleen Byrne, a consultant psychiatrist at St Fintan's Hospital, Portlaoise, the majority of suicide victims were known to be psychiatrically ill. The late Dr Kelleher, one of the experts on suicide, wrote in 1998 that the majority of those under the age of sixteen who commit suicide are male and the vast majority die from hanging. Another startling revelation is that between 50 - 70 per cent of suicides die on the first attempt, and many of them have never sought any assistance. In Japan, there have been incidences of elementary school children committing suicide because they feared their grades would not be satisfactory. In November 1999 in Scotland, a ten-year-old boy hanged himself with his school tie from the bunk bed in his bedroom after an argument with his mother about staying overnight at a friend's house.

Females tend to have more of a facility for seeking help if they feel life is getting them down. Males miss the signs which indicate to themselves that they are in trouble and in need of psychological or spiritual assistance, or else note those signs, blame themselves for their incompetence and inability to cope and head straight for extinction. The rising number of young males committing suicide indicates very strongly how society is failing them. The macho male image, personified all about them, may be acceptable when life is joyous or raucous but where are the models for how to resolve inner conflicts or difficulties when life is not so affirming? Images of successful men are so all-pervasive that the only creative option for so many young Irish males, when faced with feelings of inadequacy, fear and anxiety, is to take their own lives.

Suicide is always a tragedy but it is particularly horrific when carried out by people who've had little life experience and therefore little opportunity yet to learn from difficulties or 'failures'. Such people, already emotionally depleted, meet this one last problem or series of difficulties with despair and hopelessness and see no way forward. Every so often a suicide occurs which appears to be in response to a relatively minor problem, such as exams or not getting on with friends. Of course, this may be the final assault for a young person already depressed and isolated but most certainly what it means is that many opportunities for intervention have already been missed. Obviously, sensitivity is required here because loved ones may blame themselves and need to be helped through that, but as a society we need to realise that no one just suddenly finds themselves facing or contemplating suicide. Many steps have already been traversed, many strands have been woven which, right up to the point of execution, could be turned around. In *Raising Cain*, Kindlon and Thompson state that often the reason symptoms of depression and loneliness are missed in males is because in meeting male stereotypical expectations they so often 'look edgy or angry, hostile or defiant'. They claim that 'stoicism and emotional reserve, or even a withdrawal into his fortress of solitude are accepted and sometimes admired male behaviours'. As these authors see it, combine depression and the shame of that, with an inability to either understand what's happening or express it (emotional illiteracy) and include a natural impulsiveness with a familiarity with violence obtained via the media, and the recipe is there for suicide.

If suicide is the major statement of distress from young men, eating disorders continue to be predominantly the domain of the pubescent female. Eating disorders are on the increase with obesity now becoming a problem in Britain and Ireland. In 1986 Susie Orbach wrote *Hunger Strike*, a study of anorexia nervosa and bulimia. Within a society which objectifies femaleness and the female form, she saw eating disorders as a metaphor of the pain of women but also a response to the curtailment which women experience in every sphere of their lives. 'Whenever women's spirit has been threatened, she has taken control of her body, an avenue of self-expression. The anorectic refusal of food is only the latest in a series of women's attempts at self-assertion which at some point have descended directly upon her body.'

By the 1990s, when Naomi Wolf wrote *The Beauty Myth* little had changed. Women had more money but were using it to continually change their physical bodies. Plastic surgery was on the increase with greater and greater perfection being sought, despite health risks. As one Californian woman described to me recently, 'It's become like having braces on your teeth as a teenager, everyone has a few tucks here and there by the time you're 45 or 50.' And so women continue mercilessly to emulate some elusive vision of female beauty whatever the cost. Likewise, women continue to die from anorexia despite analysis, despite psychological assistance. Quietly and ragefully they slip from existence and so the battle on the female body continues. Germaine Greer named it succinctly when she said, 'women are illusionists', constantly trying to create some image out there of what they are. 'They fake light-heartedness, girlishness and orgasm; they also fake the roses in their cheeks, the thickness, colour, and curliness of their hair, the thinness of their waist, the longness of their legs and the size and shape of their breasts.'

This is the world our young women and men inhabit. Interestingly women are more likely to want to change their bodies and men are more likely to feel their bodies are okay, although an increasing fragility is creeping into the male experience. According to Naomi Wolf, although adult men and women are overweight in equal proportions, only one man in ten is 'strongly dissatisfied' with his body, while one-third of women are 'strongly dissatisfied' with theirs.

A further complication is that it's become quite fashionable to eat strangely – extremes are in, and eating nothing or gobbling voraciously can both be 'cool' topics of conversation. Combine this fad with fast foods and junk food and young people can be seriously undernourished, prone to illness, fatigue, depression, irritability or mood swings. Most of the super-models they seek to emulate are seriously underweight and are often themselves trapped in this fad-type eating or some other dysfunctional pattern of food consumption.

Food deprivation or anorexia is one end of the food issue and obesity is at the other end with bulimia somewhere in the middle. All are to do with an essential life element – food. All have an effect on body size and image, all express deep inner unhappiness and all can be life-threatening. The level of anxiety created in those responsible for young people is usually a result of this threat, as is also the sometimes brutal interventions which are perpetrated upon the sufferers. Frequently the carers are themselves so frightened and anxious that that becomes the main motivating force. But continual intervention means that the sufferer never gets to go through a process with it. They are deemed to be ill, in danger, not in a position to make decisions for themselves, and therefore intervention is warranted. In the case of the anorectic every time the person goes to a certain weight loss, intervention occurs and this keeps the cycle going.

Other conditions, perhaps not as serious, such as panic attacks, phobic or obsessional behaviours and sleeplessness, may also be deemed sufficient to warrant intervention or medication. While these conditions may be terrifying, it is important that other methods of assistance are attempted. If children are living in difficult situations, currently experiencing trauma or abuse, it may be that the symptom is not the problem but the circumstances. I've worked with vast numbers of adults who were victims of childhood abuse and all displayed at that time an array of symptoms such as those listed above, but for all of them that was not where the problem lay.

Symptoms of anxiety such as school phobia or school refusal are equally distressing to the child or the teenager. School refusal is very often associated with:

a) not wishing to leave the security of home and face the world;

b) fear of what is going to happen at home in their absence, such as a mother being beaten by her partner and the child fearing for her well-being or the child fearing abandonment;

c) that the mother or primary parent will leave.

School refusal is often accompanied by other symptoms of anxiety. School phobia usually is to do with difficulties in school; minor difficulties can have become exacerbated or there can be a combination of factors. Obviously, information is the best place to start. If information can't be gleaned from the child, then other sources should be investigated – teachers, other members of the family, other parents and so on – until you get a picture of the child's day in school. Something is causing the problem but it may not be anything as major as you think. Obvious possibilities such as bullying, fear of a teacher, not having friends, self-consciousness about undressing for sports, not feeling very competent, and being shy should all be considered, but it may be something less serious. Somatic stomach pains can often accompany school phobia or school refusal.

Nocturnal enuresis – bedwetting – is considered abnormal if it persists regularly after age five/six. It is sometimes accompanied by sleeplessness as the child is anxious about not wakening when he/she needs to. I've spoken with many people who were bedwetters into late childhood/early teens, and all would associate it with fear and trauma. For many this would have occurred in boarding-school, with the attendant shame of others knowing about it. Nowadays shaming is certainly not part of the cure but behavioural conditioning is sometimes meted out by the family GP in the form of stars for night dryness. Unfortunately, the anxiety or fear may be ignored. Left unaddressed the symptom may disappear but the underlying anxiety may resurface later in a different symptom. Children are fragile beings and their world can become insecure quite easily.

Particular illnesses and conditions associated with anxiety such as asthma, a wide variety of allergic reactions, and eczema are seriously on the increase. According to research published in 1998 Irish children experience a comparatively high incidence of asthma. Professor Richard Beasley from Wellington, New Zealand found that 42 countries, the highest incidence of asthma occurred in Ireland, Britain, Australia and New Zealand. The Asthma Society of Ireland states that more than 225,000 people in Ireland are affected by asthma, half of whom are children, and that asthma causes more than 100 deaths a year. While environmental factors continue to be seen as relevant, there is also some research to indicate a connection between asthma and anxiety; up to 43 per cent of asthmatic children could have anxiety disorders, according to the DSM-111-R criteria.

Learning difficulties such as dyslexia also receive considerable attention. Some children are deemed to have specific learning difficulties and require special teaching methods. While there is no doubt that children receiving extra, caringly given, teaching will benefit, I don't know if it's always a good idea to give it a name or to name the child as being different. In a way, every child has some degree of learning difficulty, every child has individual needs and every child has specific requirements. According to the Association for Children and Adults with Learning Difficulties in Ireland, dyslexia is a genetic condition, caused by differences in the way the brain functions. It runs in families and is more common in males. It is the belief of that organisation that it is not caused by emotional disturbance or family problems and cannot be the result of bad or ineffective teaching. Their understanding is that it affects approximately eight per cent of the population and that perhaps half of those will need intervention. This means that one or two children in each class may have some type of learning difficulty. Generally, children are seen to be experiencing learning difficulties when they have received normal educational input, are of normal intelligence, have been placed in an appropriate class in terms of their age, do not have any physical impairments in eyesight or hearing abilities and yet do not appear able to understand or retain basic concepts of numeracy and literacy.

The work of such organisations is positive in that it focuses on the child's needs and assures those with any level of learning difficulty that their problem is not to do with lack of intelligence or willingness to work. Annually, 840 children use their out-of-school services which are for students aged seven to eighteen years. They also offer summer schools which accommodate children not included in this figure, and a further 1,000 students, approximately, attend their service for private tuition.

There is no doubt that life experience either facilitates or inhibits a child's openness, curiosity and desire to learn, and certainly children suffering from trauma may experience little interest in learning and display little capacity for taking in new concepts. Children's ability to learn may be arrested or become dormant. It is clear that such children will need assistance. A loving, warm, enthusiastic teacher can achieve a great deal in one year or two with such a child. Equally, further and further damage can be done if an awareness of the child's problem is not incorporated into the relationship and adequate encouragement and assistance offered. To expect such a child to manage with a large grouping would be cruel. But even for ordinary children, learning must occur within the context of their personalities. Every child learns differently, at an individual pace and style which is unique to her. A teacher's skill needs to encapsulate this understanding.

Child violence requires attention. In 1993 two boys, both aged eleven, were found guilty of the murder of two-year-old Jamie Bulger in Liverpool. Horrified adults heard of the last hours of the two-year-old's life and sought to understand how this could have happened. Words like 'evil' and 'monsters' resounded in the media. The 1990s equally saw a spate of classroom and high school killings in the United States. Violence perpetrated by children and teenagers against each other is on the increase. The greater part of violence is perpetrated by male children and teenagers, either alone or in groups. Silly, meaningless quarrels develop into serious life-threatening situations with amazing speed when spurred on by alcohol or some other mood-altering substances. Violence in films and video games is blamed excessively, although there is no doubt that exposure to violence in the media desensitises the young person.

Many factors contribute to this violence. Kindlon and Thompson state in *Raising Cain*, 'Boys draw harsh discipline like a magnet and thereby learn lessons of shame and domestic violence: as teenagers, they drink sooner and harder, and drive drunk more frequently'. Clearly, boys need to be given a much wider repertoire of responses to situations which threaten them physically or psychologically. This means educating them about

109

their emotional lives, showing them that aggression should not be the first response when dealing with conflict and that overall, the world is not a threatening, hostile environment to which they must continually respond with aggressive force.

On a much lower level of violence are bullying and criticism which many children endure for years, always in some way blaming themselves for what is happening. Primary school programmes exist now which seek to address the matter. Mostly, though, the programmes will only be carried out with the children in relation to other children and not in relation to the classroom dynamics, or working with the school as a system where bullying may be occurring at different levels. Also, the bully is frequently seen as a person who can clearly be identified and of course that may be the case, but seeking the 'bully' within each person might be the most productive way to operate such programmes. If children can identify where they are bullied and where they bully themselves, then you are beginning a process of awareness with them from which to work on fairness and justice later. To fully understand the concept of injustice children need awareness; awareness of themselves, when/how they can be hurt and what that experience is like, and the feelings they have when they hurt someone. Exploring such difficult and hidden feelings may be awkward, embarrassing, even shaming, but it will also prove to be freeing for children. Both sides of the discussion need to be explored – the victim and the perpetrator – in order to offer an opportunity for unexpected discussions to emerge. Doing role-plays can encourage insights, offer some distance from the topic and also be inclusive of views which the children might be too intimidated to articulate.

The world that children and teenagers live in is filled with anxiety and they must face many threats to their sense of self. Children need to be loved and guided through the maze of difficulties they encounter, all sufficiently important to present a threat to them. As David Smail says in *Illusion and Reality – the Meaning of Anxiety*, 'There is no doubt that, in facing life's difficulties, it helps to be loved. When the gaze of the other becomes warm and approving, when we are confirmed as good, or as beautiful, the freezing winds of isolation and despair give way to a glowing self-confidence ...' If children can find this reassuring love within the parental relationship they are much less likely to find themselves in upsetting, disturbing, irresolvable conflicts in the classroom or with peers, in compromising, inappropriate liaisons in teenage years or in troubled, dysfunctional adult relationships where their sense of self is further damaged. It isn't possible to protect our children from life's difficulties, nor would it be appropriate, but it is possible to equip them more fully for the wide variety of encounters they'll be asked to contend with.

Chapter 7

TYPES OF CHILDMINDING

CRÈCHES

Childcare provision in Ireland is unco-ordinated, variable in quality, difficult to find and predominantly provided by females. To date, state expenditure on childcare has been largely in disadvantaged areas. In Budget 2000 a £46 million childcare package was given, but no tax relief for parents who pay for childcare was conceded. The cost of childcare to parents, proportionate to average earnings are amongst the highest in the EU. Average full day-care prices in Ireland are twenty per cent of average earnings and are continually on the increase. Crèches provide most of the day-care available. Crèches/nurseries provide group care for children, generally from the age of three months. The National Children's Nurseries Association was formed in 1988 to co-ordinate and bring together the providers of these services. In 1998 NCNA had approximately 400 services registered who together were catering for 13,000 children between 0 and 6 years. It is, I'm sure, correct to assume that this figure has increased since.

The childcare (Pre-School Services) Regulations 1996, require adherence to minimum standards of safety, premises, facilities and maintenance of records. While these regulations have generally been met with approval, at a time of optimum need services are closing because they cannot fulfil these requirements, leaving a greater gap between the provision of services and demand. Obviously guidance and financial assistance must be part of such regulations. In the Mid-Western

Health Board's review of such services, two-fifths of services which closed did so because of an inability to respond to inspection findings. The working group set up by the Department of Health and Children to monitor the implementation of the regulations found many areas where the standard wasn't sufficiently high, such as lack of space, insufficient staffing, insufficient toys and stimulation, poor nutritional provision, lack of sterilisation and other hygienic procedures. It is encouraging that for the first time such services are being inspected and that childcare service providers are obliged to notify an authority regarding their service. The quality of experience or training is not assessed, apart from the recommendation of 'appropriate experience in caring for children' and/or 'appropriate qualification in childcare'. Yet this process marks the beginning of strong improvements being sought, consistently monitored and implemented.

Childcare training has been somewhat haphazard and standards vary greatly. In 1997/1998 up to 4,000 people were enrolled on childcare courses. Childcare has not been viewed very positively; generally pay is low, status is also and a career path or structure does not exist. As with much work provided predominantly by women, childcare remains unorganised and lacking in any kind of positive public profile. Yet we all agree how significant that work is and how important it is that it is done by people who are skilled, happy, gaining job satisfaction, and receiving financial remuneration for their efforts. Developing a philosophy regarding childcare requires time and commitment and cannot simply be learned from theory. Ideally, in order for a crèche to function well as a service it needs to be inclusive of the workers' ideas and see them as a resource. Long-term commitment needs to be nurtured in order to foster that resource. Turnover of staff is high, particularly at the junior level. As stated earlier, nurseries/crèches provide group care for children aged from three months. Official figures stated in July 1998 that there were approximately 400 nurseries, catering for approximately 13,000 children from newborn to six years.

The average number of places per centre was 42 and the majority of children were cared for full-time. As more women return to employment, this figure will continue to grow.

While parents find the cost of crèches high, it isn't possible for people running these services to pay higher salaries. They themselves, after expenses, may not be earning a reasonable salary for the level of responsibility they are required to take. Junior staff earn about £130-£140 a week (averaging £3-£5 an hour for a 40-hour week) and senior staff earn from £160-£200 a week (averaging £4-£5 per hour for a 40-hour week. Owners and managers may earn a little more; 80 per cent of centres are owner-managed according to a survey carried out in 1998. Due to the low profit margins, part-time placements and places for babies have become harder to locate. The Regulations quite rightly require higher staff ratios for babies and this costs the manager of the childminding centre more. This is equally the case with part-time placements; the staff must be there to care for them, but the service won't be receiving a full week's payment for that child. Often, in order to maintain a place, parents have to pay for the full week even though they may be using the service for less than that.

Due to the factors listed above there is probably little time or funding for on-going training, assessment days, feedback sessions, etc. This may mean that the philosophy and basic attitudes of childcare workers vary hugely. A crèche may have procedures in place for practical routines but few guidelines regarding attitudes and philosophy of childcare, which most parents would agree were as important as, or more than, the provision of the practical amenities. Certainly, the most successful childminders are those who find it easy to be with children, enjoy them, are able to be physically demonstrative, encouraging and have fun with them. In other words, someone who has a fairly relaxed personality, who has a high tolerance for frustrating circumstances and is blessed with a sense of humour tends to be the kind of person who is good around children. The potential minder may embody these qualities but not be as efficient as you'd like in the practical domain. You have to become clear on what is most important to you; for example, you may want to ensure that your child will be physically safe, so that's your starting point. Childminders vary greatly in character and personality and particular people may appeal to you more than others. At the very least you need to feel a level of respect and trust in the childminder. They must be able to show that they can be consistent in their attitude and caring and never feel entitled, however frustrating the circumstances, to shake or physically chastise a child. Corporal punishment in crèches is not permitted.

However, one doesn't need to be physically cruel in order to be neglectful. Simply not paying attention to the child's needs or being aware of something can cause problems. Anyone watching would clearly be able to discern that the adult wasn't being attentive to the child's needs, but if it was being recounted to you it might be more difficult to identify a problem. There are a number of crèches around where I live and I frequently view interactions between the workers and the children. What strikes me most, and it is precisely the same for teachers of young children, is that when there is more than one worker, the child seems to have less possibility of being engaged with. The workers or teachers are keenly interested in interacting with each other, to the deficit of the adult-child rapport.

HOW DO PARENTS CHOOSE WHICH CRÈCHE TO USE?

During the pregnancy, consider your options and begin to investigate services. Number one priority is very often trying to find a crèche close to your home or work, as commuting in traffic may be a problem. However, this may not be the best way for you to proceed. Speak to people who are parents and have used a crèche. Speak to your relatives to ensure that you are not overlooking possible minders, and ask their advice regarding things to be aware of. Fear of asking advice, usually because one anticipates interference, can mean that wisdom built on years of experience within families may not be utilised; sometimes young parents feel they have to learn it all themselves. Both parents then need to sit down together and work out their priorities, the minimum standard / facility they would be happy with and from that, what are the questions they need to ask. Don't be put off if your initial investigations are disappointing. Equally, do not panic about the sparsity of services and feel that you must decide immediately or the place will be taken. Making a decision under such pressure is bound to be faulty. Don't be harassed into a decision but equally, be fair – don't book two places, then cancel one at the last moment. This is someone's work or business you'll mess up. They deserve notice of all changes in arrangements.

GUIDELINES
• Check out amenities.
• Check out ratio of staff to children.
• Check out length of employment of staff or length of contract they are currently on.
• Check out routines of the day.
• Is there outdoor space?
• Are they registered?
• Will they contact you if there's any problem?
• Can you speak to other parents? (Or perhaps you already know someone who has a child there.)
• Check out philosophy regarding children.
• Can the parents have any input in terms of suggestions or of being there sometimes?

ADVICE
Do not look for perfection – you won't find it. Provided you are a fairly loving parent, no one will mind your child in as good a manner as you will, because you'll be caring for your child in the context of the loving relationship which has already been established. At the same time, most people have a natural responsiveness to babies and young children who give a lot of love in return. But also listen to any hint within yourself that

either you or the child may not be happy. There are things which niggle parents, particularly women, which they never listen to, remaining in a constant purgatory of blame and guilt. They think it's simply an unchangeable facet of working outside the home. I'm saying if you have such nigglings, listen to them, understand what they mean and change that aspect of the current arrangements. You will want to believe the person you are leaving your child with is the best you can find, and that may mean that you will ignore anything you are unhappy about for fear it will lead to having to make some changes. Do not ignore anything but discuss your concerns with the staff. Very often things can be worked out. If you choose to ignore one difficulty, you may ignore another, and within no time you have a crisis on your hands and have to respond urgently. This is not what you or your child need. It takes time for the child to adapt to the minding situation, and you will not wish to swipe that away unnecessarily due to a difficulty in communication. At the same time, if you are a first-time parent you may be riddled with concerns, so check out the problem with your partner or a friend before discussing it with the service, if you feel unsure. If you query and question constantly in a bothersome way, you may then not be taken seriously when you need to be. It's better to address your worries with people who know you well, and who will understand the context of your concerns. Then, if necessary, you can check it out further.

HOW WOULD YOU KNOW IF YOUR CHILD WASN'T HAPPY?

The very first thing to realise is that you mightn't. Even being alert and well-intentioned, you may miss the signs that tell you your child isn't content and may only hear later when the child is older and verbally capable of expression. This is the risk you take when you decide to have your child minded; you are putting the child outside the sphere of care given by you or your partner, and will have to locate a high level of trust in the person you are handing your child over to.

Most important, if things are not working, is to establish

your own sense of security. Parents are very often frightened to consider this because they fear not finding alternatives. Unfortunately, sometimes the discovery or confirmation of the unsuitability of a service can arrive quite suddenly. It is extremely important to have some back-up situation which could be used temporarily, such as a family member or a friend who would assist for a short period while alternatives are being researched. Reassure yourself that the most important thing is that the child feels happy and secure, and that you will find other options if the current arrangement doesn't suit. Frequently I've encountered situations where parents weren't able to see that something wasn't good for their child because their own ego was too fragile. To have to reassess a choice already made takes courage, and parents can feel blamed or criticised, even when the realisation that things are not working so well is actually positive because now things will change.

Over-anxious parents can miss out on the assessment period necessary to estimate if an arrangement is working. A particular crèche or minder is deemed at the beginning of the relationship to be perfect, there is a fall from grace and then suddenly the child is withdrawn from that care because it's decidedly awful. Winnicott coined the phrase 'good enough mother' a long time ago, and maybe the 'good enough carer' also needs to become a reality. If you can bear in mind the difficulties the childminder encounters, and then estimate whether the minder is good enough, your decision will be more reasonable. Think of yourself as a parent, being observed and assessed, and ask yourself how you would fare? Many parents might not fare much better than the childminder, but parents always forgive themselves because they feel they love the child.

Small things may tell you the arrangement isn't working, but bear in mind that there may not be anything wrong with the childminding arrangement apart from the child wanting more of the parent's love, attention and time. Upsets, crying and clinging behaviour could indicate either possibility and you just need to realise the baby isn't happy and query what changes could be made. Remember, if you wait long enough the child will adapt, because what other option will he/she have? But this is not an appropriate or responsible response from a parent trying to offer the best possible options to their child. Changes in a baby's mood or personality, anxiety in a toddler, evidence of fear, must all be taken note of, but it is only in the overall context of knowing a child intimately that one can assess if something is amiss. When a child is verbal, listen carefully to what they tell you. Ensure that you can be open to hearing when it concerns the minder or teacher. Take very strong note of illnesses or psychosomatic disorders; it may be the only way the child can communicate. It is serious if it is being expressed in this way, but again it may not be that anything awful is happening, but that the child is seriously upset, and this must be realised.

Parents are walking a tightrope, needing to keep a lot of factors in mind. One must not err on the side of carelessness, but undue anxiety may be transmitted to the child and equally cause problems. The first and foremost question is for the parents to decide clearly what they want and what they will be happy with. If there are differing opinions then that must be worked out so that each parent can fulfil what he/she believes is right. It can be particularly difficult if parents disagree on the amount of time the child should spend in a crèche. Arguments can descend to the level of, 'Well, if you don't want your child in a crèche then you stay home'. In one such situation a woman was working four days a week, then changed to three days and two evenings and wanted her husband to cut his work down to four days a week, so that the children would be minded only for two days. He didn't feel able to make that move and so they continued, though somewhat unhappily on the mother's part, with three days of minding for the children. When opinions differ, it is a good idea to seek advice or sit and discuss the matter with a neutral party. Remind yourself how important these choices and decisions are; this will hopefully enable you to give it a priority in terms of time and attention.

None of this is easy and the decision about the care of your child must not be taken lightly; every aspect of it requires consideration, explanation and lengthy discussion. Seek advice if you're unsure, communicate your concerns, hear what others have to say, and most of all, do not feel you must know everything. Do not be put off if people feel you are overly fussy or demanding. If you were discussing a change of job or a move to another country, I can guarantee you you'd feel entitled to seek advice, engage in lengthy discussions and even be repetitive. This decision is much more important than these; you are deciding something which may impact upon your child for the rest of her life. Parenting is difficult, and raising psychologically healthy children is a formidable undertaking and will not be achieved easily. Frequently a difference can be achieved by introducing one other small ingredient into the equation; the difficulty is locating that ingredient. Ideally, a service should exist to assist parents in such decision-making, and support and sometimes question, if necessary, their ongoing parenting and childminding choices. Be practical, sensible, search for options and answers and then implement what you have understood. Do not buy into the trap that because you are choosing to work outside the home you'll have to settle for second-class everything – second-class care for your child, endless hours of work for yourself and your partner. You need to ensure that you have sufficient time to enjoy your child and that you have sufficient energy to engage in that enjoyment.

Childminders, nannies, children's nurses
Childminders provide day-care for both pre-school and school-going children. In the case of school-going children, they provide care sometimes before but most generally after school and during holiday time. Children are cared for either in their own home or that of the childminder. The Child Care (Pre-school Services) Regulations 1996 permit a single childminder to care for up to six children. There are no figures available on the existing number of childminders in Ireland, but a survey of childcare

arrangements, carried out by the ESRI indicated that nineteen per cent of children aged newborn to four years were minded by a childminder, and ten per cent of five to nine-year-olds. According to the Expert Working Group on Childcare, there are an estimated 37,900 childminders. Whole-day care (9am-5pm) is the most common childminding arrangement, and child-minding most commonly takes place in the minder's home. The ESRI survey also identified two other childminding categories:

a) the childminder who minded in the child's home and

b) the paid relative, but only a very small percentage utilised these forms of childcare.

Childminders, nannies and children's nurses provide a vital service in facilitating parents to go out to work. These people may not be well trained, paid a sufficient amount or understand the responsibility they are undertaking. The majority of minders mind the children in their own home, not the child's, and fairly typical is the mother who is caring for her own, sometimes older, children alongside this job. It is generally badly paid, but for the parent paying it often seems exorbitant since the parents are paying out of their often fairly average salaries.

Childminders willing to mind in the child's home are in high demand, but frequently salaries paid do not compare with those available in other areas of work. The solitary nature of the work discourages a lot of people, since many go to work for the social dimension. Other work structures are also absent, such as someone being able to assess your work on the spot, offer feedback, assist you and perhaps generally be available for a chat or discussion. All of this suggests to me that full-day care in the child's home is perhaps too difficult not just for the child, but also for the minder. If the child is minded in the minder's home, the minder's work life is eased somewhat since the normal structures of her home life haven't been interfered with. Friends will still call, other children may be returning from school or a partner may return for lunch; isolation doesn't exist within this arrangement.

Salaries for childminding, either in the minder's home or in the child's home, must adequately denote the responsibility undertaken. A great deal of payment is still made within the black economy. Everyone involved in the childcare debate agrees that the best protection for everyone is to be found in a decent salary being paid, which is taxed, with clear hours of work and tasks agreed upon between the couple and the minder.

Due to the difficulties in locating minders the majority of parents choose communal minding situations, such as crèches. The general government thrust is also to increase and improve crèche facilities, which in itself is a good thing. However, as I stated earlier, there are many advantages to the child being minded at home, in his own environment, by one adult, and it would be a pity if those advantages get submerged in discussions of training and improved facilities. Employing a childminder in your home can diminish some difficulties in both parents working outside the home, such as trying to get to work on time, dropping a baby to a crèche, and returning to a fairly untidy home. If parents are paying high childminding fees, they may not be able to afford someone to help with house cleaning.

Having a childminder in your home who will also do some household chores is a bonus. However, such matters must be explored with a minder beforehand as childminders can be exploited. Many will only be willing to undertake tasks to do with the child's welfare, such as washing-up baby utensils or cooking for a child.

The childminder/nanny who is available to mind a baby or child in the child's home is a treasure. It is important to look for a commitment of a couple of years at least – the child will form a bond with the person. Some people feel a certain buffer against this is to use nanny agencies, who can usually offer a replacement at fairly short notice. Practically speaking, this is helpful, but it won't address the attachment issue. Childminding and nanny agencies are indeed valuable, because some level of vetting has already gone on before the candidates reach you. Nevertheless, it is your responsibility to check everything again, thoroughly. Make no assumptions, phone previous employers, seek further information about any terminations of employment. Be clear on what you are looking for in a minder, be exact about hours and tasks, and offer a trial period. Give guidance on what your priorities are; if domestic chores are included, what sort of choices are you asking the minder to keep in mind? Parents frequently speak about their upset at the choices made, for example that dinner is being prepared but the baby is crying, or that the baby is asleep but the ironing hasn't been attempted. Being clear in your instructions is the best way to avoid problems. It may well be necessary for you to compromise. It will not be perfect, nobody will do it as well as yourself, but if your baby is happy and contented and that is your priority, perhaps it's worthwhile to quell your irritation about the ironing.

Childminding and nanny agencies can sometimes provide people at short notice short-term, such as a weekend or a week. If children are older such a system can work, but it is always advisable that the parents have a trust in the person provided. How can that trust be established? How can anyone ascertain a person's suitability for such a task from a brief interview before disappearing for the weekend? Similarly, parents may engage such minders for a week where a work trip abroad is necessary and they don't wish to disrupt children's routines. In such cases, both parents wish to make the trip, or one parent is the primary parent and the other isn't available for such situations. Separated couples who, during their time together, may have argued about childminding, now often have to truly set about being co-operative, otherwise their child is going to have a lot of needless hours with a minder.

For the millennium New Year's Eve, there was a clamour for minders and babysitters. High prices were sought by those willing to work the night, and some were even willing to take flights to other countries. Children were handed over to unfamiliar people so that the parents could party the night away. A national newspaper even carried an expensive advertisement from childminders willing to take babies from three months –

one year from 6pm 31 December until noon on New Year's Day. Why could such young babies not be kept with their parents on such a significant night?

Children's nurses are used fairly infrequently in Ireland, but where the mother is convalescing after a difficult birth and the family can afford it, their services may be sought. An Bord Altranais (Nursing Board) doesn't have figures for children's nurses working in the home, so the figure is probably negligible. Such a service can be useful provided the entire care of the baby isn't handed over. In cases where the mother is unable to care for the baby herself and the father has taken over, a strong enduring bond has been created with the child. It is a pity if most tasks pertaining to the child's early life are performed by someone who is not going to remain part of the child's life. Most experts agree on the importance of the parents being as strongly involved as possible in the infant's life both before the birth and immediately afterwards.

During my student days I applied for a position taking care of a six-week-old baby who had been cared for by a nurse until then. The mother intended spending some time with the baby but predominantly, both at night and during the day, the baby would be in the care of the minder. I had experience of minding children, coming from a large extended family, but having accepted the position, I seriously began to reflect on the level of care this baby required and the responsibility involved. Realistically, at nineteen, I didn't feel capable of undertaking the job and phoned and explained my position. The family were extremely grateful for my honesty but it merely encouraged them to believe more than ever that I could do the job. They were desperate to find a replacement for the nurse who was leaving, but fortunately I desisted. It taught me something about the vulnerability of parents in such a dilemma and how easily they can employ someone who isn't capable of the task. Parents can be duped, taken advantage of and unwittingly contribute to creating circumstances which are quite dangerous for their children.

Within the whole childminder scenario, minders can be exploited, parents can be lulled into false securities and children can be neglected, but ultimately in every situation it is the child who is defenceless and thereby the one who is most at risk of being hurt. As a country we must realise and take very serious account of these risks and continue to put as many safeguards in place as is feasible.

AU PAIRS

An increasing number of Irish families now utilise the services of an au pair to provide a childcare service. Predominantly, au pairs are female but some male au pairs are now being placed; I will be using 'she' because of that predominance. Au pair placements usually involve the provision of accommodation, food, inclusion within the life of the family and a payment of pocket money in return for child-minding. The average pocket money paid is about £35 - £40. The au pair can be asked to provide childminding for up to 30 hours a week, which anyone will agree is substantial. The number of hours of childminding required can, of course, vary hugely from family to family. Au pair placements, both here and abroad, are generally for a duration of one year but may be for six months. Such placements are linked, in this country and Europe, to the acquisition of competency in the language of that country, hence the usefulness of living with a family who will hopefully offer encouragement and assistance in becoming fluent. When things work out it is a highly effective way to learn a language and experience a culture. Friendships may continue with the host family for years afterwards.

There is no regulating body here to oversee the au pair situation. Ireland has not yet ratified the 1979 Council of Europe's agreement on au pair placements. There are no overall figures available, and individual agencies tend to be defensive or suspicious in response to queries. No childcare training is offered; potential au pairs complete application forms on their level of experience and placements are made on the basis of this. If the arrangement doesn't work out, then either the au pair or host family has the possibility of seeking an alternative placement, but the majority of replacements are held with for the agreed time. The variety of personality and corresponding skill encountered can be wide.

It is important to know the au pair's background, and I'm not speaking about socio-economic factors, more a general profile of her placing in her family and in life. For example, if there are things she's trying to leave behind or aspects of her background she's particularly unhappy about, then perhaps another job would be easier or more suitable. Entering an established family can be quite taxing and it's easier to do when one is of a happy disposition. After spending time in a family as an au pair, I heard from the au pair who came after me. It was really interesting to see how many observations and reactions she had to the family which were similar to my own even though, in fact, we were very different in personality. Talking to Irish au pairs who went abroad attempting to escape family difficulties, I found it uncanny how many found themselves in families where similar dynamics operated, even though the family hadn't been chosen by them. As the host family, it is important to consider what kind of personality type would best suit your family. The clearer and more specific you can be in the completion of the request form, the greater possibility there is of receiving what would be most suitable.

Au pairs in America are connected in everyone's mind with the case of Matthew Eappen. The idea of English-speaking au pairs going to America to experience the culture seems to have become linked inextricably with extensive childminding. I suggest that operating the au pair system where there is not a language to be acquired puts it very firmly in the realm of childcare. Many people feel that it has become a cheap form of childminding, open to abuses. Firstly, the young people receive no training in childminding, apart from guidelines and advice during their orientation course after they arrive. The au pairs believe they are going to be part of the family but may find that:

a) they are spending long hours alone with children and

b) they are treated very definitely as someone providing a service within that family, not as a member of it.

Apart from all the obvious difficulties, such as the au pair being away from family and friends and perhaps not having much access to other people her age, the situation of an au pair going where there is not a language to be learned, and therefore no motive for being there apart from travelling and having fun, creates further difficulties to be dealt with. The primary attraction for the young person is that the fare is usually paid, and having accommodation and employment can feel very safe. The parents of the au pair feel assured too, knowing all of this is set up. But the young person leaving home, perhaps for the first time for such an extended period, may not at all have thought about the difficulties of childminding alone and if she'll be able for it.

Parents of the au pair need also to be aware of the possible difficulties. It is important to assess your daughter's capabilities for such a task and speak at length to her about what her responsibilities will be. It can be quite a negative experience for the young person to have to return home because the placement hasn't worked out; this is perhaps wiser than staying in a situation which isn't functioning well, but it is nevertheless difficult.

Where a language is being learnt, an au pair is there for a very specific purpose. Living in a family environment which is encouraging and supportive of that aim has been found to be beneficial. The au pair has language classes to attend, offering the containment of a specific learning situation. Wishing to acquire the language, the au pair is in constant communication with the family. She doesn't want to waste her time. There is a specific reason for being there, a specific task on hand, and what is required from her is to be helpful within the family and provide some childminding. This means that the overall situation has a greater prospect of working, with both sides being happy with their part of the deal. Communication will hopefully remain more open and if difficulties arise there may be a strong motivation to resolve them. Au pairs said that when situations were difficult because of the desire to achieve what they had set out to do they attempted to be as co-operative as possible, knowing it was for a specific length of time. Often they managed to turn around circumstances and by the time they were leaving had acquired further perspectives on the situation.

So what is it like for the children in the au pair situation? Firstly, no matter how good it is and how successfully it works, the arrangement will end in a year. Few families succeed in holding onto au pairs for longer than that. There's going to be a loss incurred. The relationship may have been valuable but now the child has to move on and form another bond. I suggest that children from nine or ten onwards can manage this, but not babies, and unfortunately au pairs are most frequently used where there are very young children. The services of au pairs are frequently sought because the family home will be their home, therefore they can be relied on for peculiar hours of minding, such as very early in the morning or late at night, or irregular hours. With a young baby one cannot leave the house at all even for the shortest time so having someone there, available for such times, can ease matters. If the au pair is spending a lot of time with a baby or young child, then that child will become emotionally attached and it will be a wrench when the au pair leaves.

One French family I stayed with during my student days changed au pair every six months. The child, then aged five, had simply had one au pair after another and refused to relate to the au pair any longer by name. She was simply 'la jeune fille'. He was a sweet, loving boy but too many losses had made him see the au pair as nameless, someone who would leave in time and be replaced by another *jeune fille*. The hard-working professional couple concerned, who both worked outside the home, were of course trying to do the best for their children. They had older children and in previous times had employed minders who were generally immigrants and usually from a different class background to themselves. They found the workers hadn't been very good to the children and, according to the family, had 'an attitude' towards French people which didn't help matters. Their values sometimes conflicted with the family, in terms of attitudes to child rearing and other matters. Therefore they decided to opt for a transient au pair system. They were a responsible host family, kindly and keen to be of assistance, but what was happening to their child within this arrangement seemed awful.

Some mothers I spoke to in Ireland actually saw the transience of the au pair as positive, because such a system wouldn't interfere with the bonding between mother and child. Different au pairs would come and go and the mother would remain clearly the long-term carer. Obviously, this works if the mother is spending more time with the child than the au pair is. But if most of the child's waking hours are spent with the au pair and most of the child's needs are met in that relationship, clearly there is going to be confusion for the child.

Many au pairs excel in the care they give to the children in their care. These in turn form strong attachments to them and are indeed sad to see them leave. However, while au pairs may be irresponsible and neglectful, it is also true that host families can and do abuse the au pair. She can be expected to take responsibility for young children whom she doesn't know well very soon after her arrival. The au pair is generally young, late teens/early twenties, and may not actually be capable of taking such responsibility. Being required to take care of children and do housework for up to 30 hours a week is excessive. That level of responsibility would require fairly solid experience with children and maturity about life. If the au pair is being exploited financially, and you must be your own guide for this, it is not simply enough to say this guideline is provided by an agency. Do you think it's fair? If you consciously exploit the au pair for childminding purposes, then you have little grounds for complaint if things go wrong. Do keep in mind that it is your children who will bear the brunt if something is not working. I suggest that the ideal way for the au pair to earn her keep would be to help with the childminding, perhaps twenty hours a week, but mostly when one of the parents or another adult family member is in the house. Never, never should your children be left for all-day, overnight or weekend care with the au pair. Parents find such long-term care exhausting; how can a young person with no strong relationship to that child be expected to cope? It is simply being irresponsible both to the au pair (who is also somewhat in your care) and to the children.

The au pair system can and does work well for people where the family are very reasonable in their expectations, fair childminding is expected, and the au pair is given assistance to settle in, get to know the country and enjoy her stay. To the person merely seeking a solution to childcare this may seem like too much work, and perhaps it is. It is important to consider the input you are going to be obliged to have at the beginning to set the arrangement in motion, and how you will need to constantly be aware of the au pair's needs throughout the stay. In a way, the host family is placed in a quasi-parental role.

Having an au pair can provide for children a lovely experience of people from another culture, once the au pair clearly remains in a helper category to the parents and not a replacement one. The experience can be enriching for the children, rather than something which shakes their security. The children will often wish to remain in contact with the au pair, communicating by letter or email. Situations such as the au pair coming for one year first and then returning for summer months for a couple of years after that seemed to work wonderfully. Everyone involved had a very positive experience – the parent at home received help and company, the children had the opportunity to receive an acceptable amount of minding by another adult who lived in their home, and the au pair had a family to live with, a home-away-from-home, in exchange for some work.

BABYSITTERS
Babysitters are generally engaged for periods of time in the

evening while the parent or parents socialise or attend to other matters. The work usually involves putting the child to bed, reading a story, settling the child for the night and continuing to care for him until the parents' return. This is, of course, the ideal situation. The reality can be somewhat different. Bedtimes may be particularly difficult for some children, in a time of unease or fear. They may be unhappy about the babysitting or the parent going out, and need reassurance. Unfamiliarity with a babysitter can ensure that the child will not adhere to the normal routines. A child can wake upset, and need comforting. Babysitting can, and often does, involve taking care of a baby who is ill, distraught or simply chooses not to sleep. Because babysitting generally occurs in the evening, when children are expected to sleep, the idea exists that it is a simple task to be undertaken by the young and unskilled. The younger the child, the greater the skills required, can be offered as a general maxim. But older children also require someone who can clearly take charge in a calm and assertive matter. Unexpected things can happen. The babysitter needs to be able to cope with all probabilities. Extra children may be being minded. Children who are normally well behaved can become energetic little fiends and make life hell for a babysitter, who then becomes frustrated and behaves equally badly, yelling or offering threats.

Parents need to be sensible about babysitting. Do you require it? If you have one child, a baby, can you take the baby with you to the social event? Check with your host/hostess, restaurant owner, hotel manager, or relevant person. If a babysitter is required, that decision and choice requires as much attention as any other aspect of your child's care. The person must be familiar to the child beforehand and be brought to play with, or take care of, the child in your presence a few times before the arrangement commences. Both the babysitter and the child/children can mutually benefit if the babysitting is well organised and parents adhere to their side of the bargain. It can be an event the child looks forward to and welcomes because of the activities, interests or fun it brings. On the other hand, children need to be prepared beforehand; it should not be just sprung on them at the last moment, as this is unfair to everyone involved.

Regarding the age of the babysitter, a number of factors must be taken into account such as the age of the child, whether there are any particular requirements, whether there is more than one child and the length of time it is generally for. It is probably true to say that fifteen is the minimum age at which one can become responsible for the care of others in a restricted way. A fifteen-year-old, if mature, is capable of babysitting, but not for a prolonged time. I suggest that would require a seventeen/eighteen-year-old. Can the person be responsible about the house? Is the person actually capable of overseeing things? I'm constantly appalled by how easily strangers are given this job, particularly if the regular babysitter is not available. Teenagers, not known to either parents or children, are brought in at the last moment because a social event can't be cancelled. Putting your child in anyone else's care is always risky and due account needs to be taken of this. Children have been frightened, terrorised, physically and sexually abused and even killed by babysitters, so it is not a job to be offered lightly to teenagers, nor accepted lightly. Those wishing to put themselves forward for such work must like children and be comfortable with them. Parents of teenagers wishing to offer such a service would be wise to explore with them their capabilities, the possible dangers, and remind them of considerations such as clarity about times and payment, arrangements about returning home, cooking and so on.

Parents employing a babysitter need to give and obtain clear information on all of the following:
- Payment – how much per hour and does the rate change after a certain time.
- Transport to house and home again.
- Availability of parent to be contacted when out – number of mobile phone or place of contact.
- Back-up contact if cannot reach parent. Are the babysitter's

own parents available for advice, or another contact?
• Clarity regarding discipline so no misunderstanding can arise.
• Smoking – what is your position?
• Use of alcohol – is it allowed?
• Clearing up of toys used or food consumed.
• Use of phone.
• Bringing a friend or boyfriend/girlfriend.

It is important as a parent to outline your philosophy regarding childcare and your child so that the babysitter can formulate some notion of what will be expected. Also, it helps to alleviate any possible misunderstanding regarding how the child may be treated.

The ideal situation is where someone can remain a babysitter for a number of years. It's also important to remember how many extra people are already involved in the child's life. How many minders is he/she encountering per week? The aim, particularly throughout the early years, is to create as much stability as possible, so the fewer minders the better. Naturally that can be increased as children get older. If the babysitter in the evening is the same minder as the day-time that's a bonus. Equally, if it can be a relative whom the child is familiar with that's an advantage. It can present a valuable opportunity for, say, a grandparent to spend time every week with that child. As communities, in many ways, continue to disintegrate it is encouraging to see the number of grandparents who nowadays choose to involve themselves in the care of their grandchildren, minding them during the day, collecting or delivering them to school or taking them to activities after school. Another possibility for babysitting is a teenager within your extended family. You'll have the advantage of knowing the young person, being acquainted with his/her personality and suitability before you even suggest it. The next best option is a friend's or neighbour's child, as there is at least some familiarity with the family and thereby some structure for accountability exists. The least recommended decision is to choose someone you don't know, but of course this may well be necessary. In this case, offering the opportunity for the babysitter to become familiar is essential. Very often, parents put great efforts into locating responsible minders for the daytime and fail appallingly regarding babysitting at night because of the irregularity of that requirement.

With regard to young babies, it's appropriate to have them with you as much as possible as long as you realise that you'll be the one responsible. It's unfair to expect others to take care of the baby; they may be willing to help but that's different from you, as the parent, entering the situation with that expectation. Babies, when young, ideally should spend the least amount of time necessary away from their parents.

If parents are working outside the home during the day, where social situations can include the children, regardless of age, so much the better. If activities at weekends can encompass friends with their children everybody can be accommodated. It will mean the social life of a couple with children will be different from those who don't have children, but that perhaps is appropriate. Too often, children are kept separate from events and activities involving the parents. This is not to deny that the parents need time on their own as a couple but this time perhaps can be a late evening meal together or an early morning breakfast. Babies can be left in the care of others for an extended time far too early because the couple need time to themselves. All the time, it is important to estimate how much time the child is spending with each of the parents. It's not sufficient to estimate, for example, that since the baby has been with the mother all day it is acceptable for both parents to go out that evening. Both parents must, in turn, estimate their time with the child and question whether it is sufficient to form and maintain a strong bond.

Travelling for work or pleasure it is preferable to take children under four to five years with you and also take a babysitter. It will present further complications in organisation, but you'll be available to the child for at least some time during the trip. Work trips away from home are sometimes an opportunity for parents to get time away from the chaos of family life, but I suggest the cost for the child is too high. Short spells away from a child can help to rejuvenate lagging energy and spirits and won't usually pose a difficulty for the child. Obviously, if your work trip is abroad it will prove to be more costly to take a babysitter and baby with you, but maybe companies need to begin to pay for such necessities when parents travel. Naturally partners could fulfil such a facilitating role if they were available. I've seen friends be incredibly creative in their decisions about travel, work and children. Part of the problem arises when parents try to separate the roles of parent and worker. Family life has had to make constant concessions to the working life of the parents, and it's time for that to become a two-way flow.

Regarding holidays, if the choice is to go without a baby or child or take a babysitter with you, it's preferable to choose the latter. You may not want a full-time minder but would like some time off in the evening, so a babysitter is a good choice. Many holiday complexes abroad provide babysitting services, but those people will be strangers to your baby and also you, as the parent, will have no familiarity with them or their style of minding. An au pair could obviously provide this service also. Holidaying abroad with a baby or children is naturally very different from being a couple on holidays. Peaceful lounging on the beach can become something you dream longingly of! This is all the more reason to think carefully about having a baby; life will never be the same again. You will never again not be a parent to this child regardless of any decisions you take, apart from giving the child up for adoption or the child later divorcing you. Taking a babysitter with you on holidays may not fulfil all your dreams of a much-needed rest, but your mind will be eased, knowing your child/children are in your care.

Where parents are separated and the child/children are living with one parent, it is a good idea if the overall arrangements can include the other parent babysitting. It means that valuable time lost with that parent can be clawed back. Few separated couples feel able to incorporate this arrangement because:

a) the full-time parent doesn't want the father (it's usually the mother who is the full-time parent) in her house;

b) the father doesn't wish to be accommodating to the mother's social life;

c) the father is living at such a distance that it isn't convenient to make the journey for a few hours with the child.

Babysitting, if thought about well by the parents and organised successfully, can be a positive experience for the child. Thinking about the requirements is just another set of tasks for the couple where both people work outside the home, and who perhaps are already feeling overburdened by the amount of organisation they must do. Yet, as with many of the other aspects of the child-minding regime, it is so important to choose well.

BOARDING SCHOOLS

After-school care is on the increase with schools providing after-school minding, extending the student's day. Equally, children are being dropped to school earlier to facilitate parents getting to work. In the past, boarding schools provided a childminding service with children returning home only during holiday time. Visiting of parents was restricted, so the children relied strongly on the staff to meet their daily emotional and physical requirements. Nowadays boarding school students return home most weekends, but it can still be argued that the schools provide a childminding service during the week. All of the daily hassles are taken out of the parent-child relationship and placed in another setting.

Boarding schools have provided the backbone of middle-class education over the past 30 or 40 years. That too is changing. The total number of second-level boarding schools in Ireland is 61; eighteen of those are boys only, eleven are girls only and 32 are mixed. 2,622 pupils attend boarding schools. Children enter secondary school boarding schools at approximately the age of twelve, but the highest attendance level is for the senior cycle. The vast majority are Catholic schools run by religious orders, i.e., single men or women living as a community and overseeing all aspects of the teenager's life for the period of the school year. Primary schools which take boarders have almost gone out of business, with only a handful of schools offering such a service. In the past this service was frequently used by diplomats and others working abroad where the schools of the country they were living in were deemed inappropriate, the work of the parents required frequent moves between countries or they wished their children to receive an Irish education. The boarding school in Ireland became the home-base, offering an Irish education while the parents travelled the world, joined by their offspring in holiday time. The fact that their children were being educated in Ireland, nurtured and maintained for the parents a strong connection back to their roots.

In Britain, boarding primary-schools still flourish, with children as young as seven or eight being sent off into the care of others. The attitude still prevails, particularly in the upper classes, that this is the appropriate route to a good education, something which both parents and children brace themselves for, because it is the 'right' thing to do. The upset which both children and parents feel at the premature separation is seen as something to be got over. It is amazing in a progressive age, when we aim to think so carefully about children's rights, that such practices continue. If a similarly aged child is taken into care, there is a great deal of emphasis put on the relationship with the parents and every effort is made to afford opportunities for the continuance of that relationship. Yet children are sent off to boarding schools and comply with hardly a murmur of dissent. They adapt, conform, do their best and usually make their parents proud of them. What is difficult to understand is that even though a child may be saying he doesn't want to go, and a parent, most frequently a mother, is feeling sad and upset about it, the arrangement still goes ahead. The people involved are feeling devastated but the idea will still be proceeded with. This seems to show that emotions are not to be trusted or included as information, in understanding what is right; as a result a vital regulation – the emotions – becomes distrusted by the children and eventually disowned. This leaves children vulnerable, and unable sometimes to read their own responses. They may not feel happy about something that is happening to them, but since they have learned to renounce the credibility of those emotions they may continue to engage in something which is harmful to them.

To create a distance for children between their emotions and an event is risky. Children need to be taught to respect their emotional responses, feel entitled to speak about them, and receive a respectful response from the adults in their lives. Frequently, adults understand this to mean giving a licence to children to do only what they want to. This is not the case. If, for example, a child indicates he doesn't wish to do something because he's frightened, he may simply be indicating he needs greater assistance to do it, greater encouragement or perhaps that smaller steps towards the task would be appropriate leading to further and further moves until the child can comfortably achieve the desired task. Placing a young child in boarding-school means that you, as the parents, are not there on a daily basis to assess progress, and you must rely on others, who do not intimately know him, for that information. Do you wish to take that kind of risk with such a precious being, your child, who has been entrusted to you?

What happens to all of the shadow aspects of their personalities? They certainly can't be dealt with by teachers who have extensive responsibilities. Such conflictual difficult emotions are hidden and will emerge later in life as dysfunctions, something aberrant and separate from the person. I believe those half-understood, conflictual emotions have their place in the long-term parent-child relationship as the child grows. Weekend visits or holiday times will not provide the length of time or intensity of relationship for difficult aspects of the personality to be manifested, acknowledged and eventually integrated in the teenage years. It is the security, strength, power and nurturance of the parental-child relationship which can facilitate such all-round growing up and maturation.

There are five strands which are bringing about change in the use of boarding schools in Ireland.

1.) With vocations to the religious orders diminishing all the time, there are difficulties in simply running the schools through lack of staff. Some have been forced to close the boarding section of the schools. Recently, the Holy Ghost fathers announced such a decision regarding their schools.

2.) Parents today, many of whom were educated in boarding schools, do not choose such an education for their children because they feel it wasn't so good for themselves.

3.) Children have more of a say in the choice of school attended and many would not choose boarding schools. I spoke to some children whose choice wasn't listened to and who were attending boarding schools because of their parents' decision. They simply had to adapt to that decision.

4.) There are a greater number of schools in rural areas, so it isn't always necessary to leave an area to find a suitable education.

5.) Due to the many scandals which have been uncovered regarding children placed in boarding school care, parents are more cautious about handing over the care of their children to others. In the past, such handing over took place under the mantle of absolute trust in the religious orders or authority figures running the schools, but this has now been eroded.

Regarding secondary school boarding, the advantages of a very structured environment with few distractions are stressed when parents are deciding on such an option. Students are required to spend a specific time of study each evening, which is generally non-negotiable. Sporting activities are close at hand and can be engaged in most days; this is a joy for the sporting enthusiast. If boarding school is being chosen as a means of curbing a wild or aggressive personality or as a way of forcing a teenager to study, this is unfair to both the child and the school which he attends. If he/she is difficult, then you as the parent must attempt to deal with those problems in the context of the parental relationship, however frustrating and irritating that is. You, as the parents, must manage it, oversee possible solutions and hopefully eventually bring about resolutions, not hand the problem over to someone else who does not have a relationship with the teenager.

The circumstances in which I have seen boarding school as a positive experience for the child are where home life is providing very little containment, or where there has been a lot of loss and bereavement in the child's life and there isn't an adult who can move in and create a secure environment for their growing up. School becomes the secure base where people can be relied on and events happen in a regular, anticipated manner. When home life is disorganised, dysfunctional, or the child is an only child spending either a lot of time alone or being moved around between minders, or a parent is travelling a lot due to work commitments, boarding school can offer a sustaining regularity of routine. A chaotic and disorganised home life can be very difficult for a child who likes order and routine. Such a child may be happy to escape to a more ordered environment. Similarly, if there is a problem of addiction or violence with one of the parents, or strong marital discord, a child will experience some freedom and relief in being able to distance herself from those problems. Obviously, the severity and deprivation of such environments would have to be dealt with, but boarding school can provide a breathing space from the tension of such an existence and offer the opportunity of experiencing another way of living.

If boarding school is used as a punishment or to solve family dilemmas (and this occurs more frequently than you might think) it can break a teenager's spirit and this is very serious. Having a truculent teenager in the house may be trying if your new partner has just moved in, but it is important to remember that one person in this equation is still a child, in need of parental protection and love, despite the protestations of independence. Being offered an option of becoming co-operative or being sent to boarding school is hardly fair. Within the formation of new relationships, children and teenagers must continue to receive priority over the adults in that situation due to their dependent status. They have been brought into the world under your guardianship, and require and deserve that protection until they can care for themselves. Care and love cannot be conditional on them behaving and being the way that you want – that means using your love, which they need, and the possible withdrawal of it, to curb their behaviour. Being a child of loving parents is the only opportunity to receive unconditional love. In adulthood, love will always be conditional, which is appropriate, since one must be responsible, and if adult life is built on a childhood of unconditional caring then things run smoothly.

In considering whether boarding school is the correct option for your child, begin by listing the things the child will gain alongside what will be now omitted or limited in his experience. What is the basis of the decision? If there are particular aims, can they be achieved by any other means, e.g., if acquiring a fluency in a language is the aim, are there any other options? Similarly, if the aim is to encourage the student to be more focused in his school work and achieve higher grades, are there other options? Consider carefully what the young person wants. Include also questions such as the impact on sibling relationships. If the school is single sex, bear in mind the consequences of spending five days a week living and learning in a predominantly single-sex environment, and be open to questioning if such an environment is conducive to creating healthy attitudes towards sexuality. Think about the various aspects of the child's personality and ask how well he'll be served. Even when the child is choosing boarding school himself, it is important to explore all of these aspects.

Finally, always remember that each child is an individual and what accommodates one child may not be suitable for another. The decision must be made individually for each child.

Chapter 8

WHAT DO CHILDREN WANT?

We know a great deal about what adult men and women want and desire. We also know a lot about what our economy needs and what companies and organisations wish to create. So what about our children? What do they want and need?

Very often parents start out with a clear notion of what they'd like to provide for their child, how they'd like that relationship to be and what, from their own background, they most certainly do not wish to replicate. As life moves on and many factors get included in the whole equation, it becomes apparent to what extent people duplicate their own experiences of childhood but under a slightly different guise so that, at first glance, it may not look at all similar. Of course, there are indeed parents who genuinely make good choices based on informed decisions, and create balanced, nurturing environments for their children. In speaking to parents, however, I was struck by the number who took extreme positions. Grouping A felt totally assured of their position, decisions and choices, and exhibited defensive responses if anything within that was questioned – their position was 'look, I know I'm a good parent'. Very little openness existed to hearing anything else, and it was possible to see how difficult it would be for the children within this family to name/exhibit any difficulties without being blamed for them. Grouping B were very open to considering how they might not be doing so well, but to such an extent that they ended up confused and willing to be led by their children without maintaining the responsibility of being the guide.

Parents continue to make decisions about the life of the family and not consult the children. Many children were not included in discussions regarding which secondary school they would attend, trips to Gaeltachts or foreign exchange student trips abroad. Neither, sometimes, were they consulted on house moves, or work trips abroad where the entire family was going. Some parents felt the children would simply have to adapt to their choices, and though somewhat sympathetic, felt that that was that.

Obviously it's difficult for parents to see their failings and shortcomings while still keeping sight of the many things they do well. That is, of course, a necessary position if one is to be open to change and to hearing what your children have to say. Speaking with children and teenagers, it was amazing how many felt they had quite a good rapport with their parents yet actually how few of their problems they would speak about to them, particularly if the issues concerned the parents and their actions. Children still fear their parents, but not always because of the parent's anger and certainly not because of any physical chastisement they may incur. They fear their parents' disappointment and/or disapproval, and mostly children strongly endeavour to do their best to satisfy their parents. As a broad generalisation, it was true to say that children and teenagers looked better in a superficial conversation than in a more in-depth exploration. For example, the children who seemed to take on challenges easily were able to indicate the difficulties and conflicts they faced when questioned. Very often children indicate they are managing much better than they actually are. Deeper exploration brings forth deeper difficulties, but if unearthed, these problems can be dealt with. If the child feels he must hide such difficulties for fear of upsetting the parents, he may learn always to conceal his vulnerabilities or aspects of his personality he needs assistance with. Such concealment doesn't build strength of character.

RESPONSES FROM ADULTS WHOSE PARENTS WORKED OUTSIDE THE HOME WHEN THEY WERE CHILDREN

What was clear in speaking to people who had grown up in this situation was that many had grown up feeling abandoned and neglected, particularly where the parents' professions demanded long hours of work and thereby absences from home. They would not have felt able to speak to their parents about these feelings, and mostly dealt with them alone. Some were comforted greatly by having good, loving attention from women who took care of them, others felt neglected in care and believed they were obliged to become independent before they were ready. Many spoke of feeling a jealousy of children where one person remained at home (usually the mother) to be the homemaker. They spoke of being in such homes, staying overnight, and feeling the comfort and closeness of that home, something that was lacking in theirs due to the frequent absence of the parents. It was clear that the regimes which the women worked within were harsh to a family system and it was probably the exception, rather than the norm, when women managed to carry the responsibilities of home and work successfully.

Those whose parents had businesses attached to the house seemed to fare better; they enjoyed some level of involvement in it and understood their parents were more available to them. There was a merging of the working and family life which was valuable. The parents just didn't disappear to work each morning; a familiarity with the parent's world was maintained. Mostly, complaints were about the chaos and confusion of their lifestyle or the expectation of inclusion within the work of the business. Their experience was that the business (usually hotels, shops, restaurants, etc.) intruded on their family life, devouring time which might have been for the family. They longed for routine hours and for the family to have time together away from work. They had little experience of family time being sacred, special or uninterrupted.

For those who grew up on farms it seemed harder to define if the mother worked outside the home or not. She didn't leave home but was involved in the farm work or the operation of it, so wasn't solely available for childminding either. Very often also the children were involved in the work of the farm, particularly as they got older. Some felt the tasks had clearly been work and were too substantial for children to be involved in. On the positive side, being involved in the farm work usually meant the opportunity to be with their father, which most people welcomed. There were occasions alone with their father which were special. However, the experience of endless chores and repetitive work was tiresome for many.

On the other hand, those whose parents went out to work felt they often had to compete with that world for their parent's attention and again felt jealous of those who were getting that attention. Most of the upset and disappointment was directed at the mother. Many seemed to miss their mothers more, something that is usually culturally encouraged. It is important to remember that this grouping had lost the immediacy of experience and have had the opportunity to reflect on their childhoods from their adult lives. Nevertheless, it is important to include, because this informed their decisions about their own childminding arrangements and their perceptions about what was important for their children.

People whose mothers had jobs where the full-time hours away from home were less than usual, such as primary or secondary teachers or third level lecturers, equally didn't feel so abandoned. Sometimes they even attended the same educational institution, which posed specific difficulties but offered the solace that their mother was available to them if necessary. It seemed their world was less fragmented; the mother was either with them in school, or was available at home for more hours than would be typical of someone working full-time. They experienced either the mother leaving and returning with them most days, or being at home when they left and returned. The returning home time seemed to be important; the most preferable option was for the mother to be there, next the minder/housekeeper, and least preferable was returning home to an empty house. Many children whose parents work outside the home return after school to empty houses. Some older children are even required to be responsible for younger siblings until the parents' return from work. Children up to the age of fifteen or sixteen years should return to situations where an adult is in charge. Even if they do not require a meal on their return, they need someone to hear about their day and generally settle them into the activities of the afternoon/evening.

Children who had a parent at home with them for the early years seemed to be more accepting of the parent's career, and claimed to have had positive experiences after the school day with relatives or minders. Mostly, such children spent evenings with their parents and that supplied a measure of contentment and ease. Those who had been minded by grandparents spoke of positive experiences and had fond anecdotes to relate. Some families experienced parental conflict because the mother was going out to work, particularly in situations where she had returned to second chance education and now was entering a new career. Such children felt proud of their mother and mostly supported her choice, which often opened opportunities later for them. Their sense of security wasn't rocked and that was crucial.

The grouping which seemed to have the most negative experience from both parents working was:

a.) where the marital relationship was strained, and

b.) where there were financial difficulties.

In such cases it seemed that the mother wasn't 'choosing' to work outside the home but was feeling obliged to and the father was blamed for this dilemma. The atmosphere was stressful and children were expected to assist in minding younger siblings and housework. Because of the circumstances, they felt obliged to comply and frequently did so resentfully, but they couldn't complain openly because the parents (and particularly the mother) struggled so hard to provide financially for them. They were caught in defending one parent against the other in the many parental disputes which occurred. These adults indicated that too much responsibility had been placed on them as children and that they had been cared for too little. They had been unable to indicate how unhappy they felt at the time because of the constancy of the familial difficulties. Returning home from school alone or returning to an empty house was normal.

The particular circumstances of parenting which these people had experienced meant that all seemed very keen not to repeat the mistakes of their parents. In some cases, the women had taken a strong stance in their relationship in terms of staying home full-time, feeling they wished to provide an experience of mothering for their children which they'd missed out on.

RESPONSES FROM CHILDREN REGARDING WHAT THEY PREFER

Predominantly, what emerged was that children and even teenagers liked their parents to be available when they needed them! So it was okay for the parents, and again, particularly for the mother, to work once it didn't intrude too much on their needs. They wanted her to be home the same time as themselves but on evenings where they remained later in school for activities, it was okay for her to not be home. Obviously, the older the child the more capable she was of understanding the need for both parents to work. The resulting financial compensations also were referenced. This grouping were more accepting of the normality of both parents working outside the home, given the fact that much higher numbers of women now do so. Some of the previous adult grouping spoken to had felt that they had been deprived of something which most people their age were receiving – tender, loving care in the home.

1.) GROUPING WHERE BOTH PARENTS WORKED OUTSIDE THE HOME

For some of these children the mother worked fewer hours than the father or other mothers worked from home. The work they were engaged in could be done there and later transferred to a central office, or they were artists who had work facilities at home. Some worked a certain number of hours, while children were minded or at school, and others worked late in the evening. Those children seemed to take that work for granted, and it had become quite integrated into their lives. Some complained a little about the summer holiday and the intrusion of work, but it didn't seem to bother them unduly. Overall, there was a distinct difference in the acceptance level of the mother working outside the home between the children/teenagers I spoke to and the previous grouping of adults, some of whom felt damaged or deprived by the experience. Mostly, I met with acceptance in the grouping currently experiencing such situations. The creativity which women put into their work arrangements was also apparent. Many had stretched work situations to suit their family's needs. Some were working for less money because of the flexibility they sought.

Where both parents were engaged in traditional working schedules the circumstances seemed more difficult. Though the majority of children did not complain of being greatly dissatisfied, some young children were indeed spending long days away from parents. They were in school for part of the day, then went to crèches or other minding facilities, or were engaged in activities after school. Many didn't see their parents until about 7pm; usually homework had to be completed by that time and if they were young they went to bed at 8 – 8.30pm. This didn't leave much time for parent-child activities. I was astonished by how 'good' these children were; they did their best with what they had and seemed to be very understanding about the parental work situation. All enjoyed days when parents were home from work, either the regular weekend days or, most especially, if either parent was free during the week. Some parents were working flexi-time and the benefits of such a system was clear. If either parent was able to finish work early, even infrequently, this had a positive impact. Being left to school, collected, or the parent returning home by 4.30pm all had positive implications. A number of small concessions in the week clearly eased the lot of children where both parents worked.

Illness caused some problems. Many wanted to be cared for by a parent when ill but this wasn't always possible. Some spoke about there being no arrangement in place for such an emergency, and one child recalled being required to go to school even though she was ill because she couldn't remain home unsupervised. Some children indicated it would be nice to return home after school, but knew it was impossible because their mother worked. They didn't even consider that perhaps they should speak to their parents about it. Somehow, the value of speaking about a problem or desire had eluded them.

When this grouping was questioned about whether they would prefer one parent home full-time, most considered it would be quite nice. The teenage grouping felt it might have advantages, but did not wish to experience a drop in living standards. They coveted what they had materially, whether it was ease with pocket money, the type of house they lived in, or their parents' cars. Some were concerned that their mothers (they presumed she would be the parent to remain home) would become overprotective. This was the case with some of their peers whose mothers were home full-time, they suggested.

For children whose parents were separated, it was obvious the system was under pressure. Where new relationships had been formed, there were now extra people to take care of them and that had positive consequences, but equally new relationships made further demands on their parents particularly if there were new step-siblings. The issue of both parents working outside the home receded in significance; such children had to contend with going between two homes, dealing with new parental partners and sometimes getting used to new siblings. They seemed more interested in focusing on these issues than in discussing both parents working outside the home.

2.) GROUPING WHERE ONE PARENT WAS HOME FULL-TIME

In the majority of these cases it was the mother who worked at home full-time. Young children appeared very content with the situation and seemed to benefit in many aspects of their lives. They felt secure in the knowledge that that parent would be at home when they returned from school. Also, they were relieved to know she'd be easily contactable at home if there was a problem or a child was ill. They liked the idea of being the primary focus and that they had their mother to themselves, as they said, for large chunks of time in the week. They all spoke fondly of their fathers but the most significant relationship was clearly with the mother: older children appeared to be conscious of the amount of mothers who work outside the home, and sought to 'excuse' their mothers for not doing so; some tendered the length of hours which the father worked or the amount he travelled as a prohibitive factor. Clearly some of these children and teenagers were somehow receiving the message that it would be preferable for their mother to also work outside the home. Culturally, things are changing. Some also spoke of the amount of after-school activities which they were involved in, requiring someone to be available to transport them to and from venues.

Most didn't get to spend much time with their fathers. Many fathers worked long hours – leaving home at 7.30am and returning at 7.30pm was not unusual. The children I spoke to accepted this mostly without complaint, proudly speaking of their fathers' work and indicating the things their fathers did with them at weekends. Many of these fathers travelled abroad for their work, and some regularly spent periods of time away from home.

Overall, what I began to understand was that precisely because things are changing, children are being asked to manage more and more in terms of their lives, even if it is only more and more activities. They seemed to accept their lot and genuinely did the best with whatever arrangements were in place. It would indeed be interesting to see what these children would have to say in ten years' time.

Chapter 9

HAVING IT ALL

In the last ten years there has been a plethora of self-help literature proposing the idea of 'having it all', each publication claim-
ing to offer a euphoric domain where one never has to say no
and compromises and sacrifices don't exist. Sounds like a three-
year-old's dream! Incantations of 'I deserve the best', 'I'm
important' and 'notice me' abound.

Of course it's important to be optimistic about life and truly
endeavour to live the best life you can; indeed, that is your
obligation. Maslow cautioned that if we deliberately set out to
be less than what we are capable of being then we will be eter-
nally unhappy. But life is also about managing options and
choices, and choosing timing. The 'having it all' idea panders to
the personality-disordered, those who are sensation-seeking,
where enough is never enough and constant change is seen as
progress. Constant change may in fact be simply holding tight-
ly in place all of the dysfunctional ways of living. Having the
staying power, tenacity and will to see something through and
face the challenges within it might, in reality, be making
progress.

It is necessary to ascertain what progress means in your life.
If it is spiritual or moral progress that is being sought, you need
to have some notions of what you mean by morality. Morality
and spirituality have become separate entities; people are
described as being very 'spiritual' yet are living lives clearly
lacking in moral strength and endeavour. Such exemptions

indicate a decline in old-fashioned ideals such as decency and kindness, conceding to such values as selfishness and self-absorption.

Is material progress part of your plan, or do you consider that spiritual or moral growth are not usually linked to material well-being? If you are attempting to 'have it all' then you truly are in need of some moral or spiritual guidance and need to assess what values you are living by. If your progression causes someone else's demise or brings about harmful consequences, clearly the path needs to be further investigated. Frequently, at this point, echoes of 'I'm not responsible for others' and 'they must choose for themselves' will be heard. The whole concept of moral progress needs to be closely monitored. Ideally, feedback from other people in your life should be invited, as people have a warped idea of their own progress; what they experience as advancement others may see as manic or destructive. One way to ensure that you are actually progressing is to use a process such as the following:

a) internal reflection,

b) engagement with others about this (it is vital that this engagement is with more than one person),

c) seeking feedback from those who are being impacted upon by your decisions,

d) further reflection.

Opportunities present constantly as part of life's development; and it is important to understand, value and be able to see those opportunities. Accepting and assessing such openings is part of joining life's flow. But it doesn't have to mean that to dash ahead is the only right thing to do simply because the opportunity is there. Opportunities will arrive again and again.

Sometimes people fear that there won't be another opportunity and they must grasp this one now. Most of the self-help literature speaks of courage in leaping forward, taking the step, doing it (whatever) despite feelings of reserve, but sometimes saying no to something can be truly courageous and the very best way to create a holistic life. If you can see opportunities, then there will always be other risks to take, other things to do. Having the ability to see the full picture is perhaps a gift. Being open to one's life and opportunities doesn't mean grabbing. It's about being flexible, trusting life's flow, being in charge but accepting that it's not all under your control. Life is always complex and there's a lot that we don't know or understand. The notion of 'having it all' can be a dangerous concept in the hands of people who are narcissistic; it gives permission to push ahead with one's desires regardless of what that means to others. The belief often is, if it's good for me, then it's good for the world. Tell that to children of ambitious parents who never thought to consider how their long hours of work, or travel away from home, would affect their children.

Alongside this is the abundance of books on women displaying superhuman qualities who can clearly 'do it all', whose lives are organised in military-like fashion in order to 'have it all'. What about the cost? Pursuing the 'have it all' or 'be it all' theory may be compulsive and addictive. One is constantly striving towards some goal, but is living being missed along the way? Women are being shown other women who need less sleep, achieve more, earn more, and so on. Women, who are already stretched in their coping capacity, begin to feel that there's something wrong with them, instead of seeing the 'craziness' and manicness of it all. Maybe some things about the life need to change, not the person. Women are too familiar with adapting, rarely stopping to consider is there something wrong with what is being asked of them. It is chilling to consider that instead of being encouraged to stop, think and assess, such women could be egged on by such literature to be more, do more, achieve more, thinking all the while that they are living their lives more fully. One woman, speaking to me recently about the constant activity and 'busyness' of her life said, 'It's hard to stop, it's as if I can't'. She was probably right; caught on that treadmill, the only way off may be to collapse.

It is important to consider what you understand 'success' to be. Is it success in someone else's eyes, such as having a lot of money or a revered job? Is it something viewed objectively by the world or is it subjective, with a very private dimension to it, something you can truly only assess yourself? By the time people have been parents for a number of years they will be faced with this question. Frequently, parents feel that success in the work domain can probably only fully be achieved by one parent while the other, if working outside the home, continues to negotiate the world of work and home life, sometimes with great compromises regarding career advancement. Everybody likes to feel productive in their life and that they are contributing to society. People like to have their talents appreciated and to receive praise, but sometimes the most important 'work' of your life may not be visible to others. You, yourself, need to have sufficient self-confidence to be able to handle that, otherwise your sense of self will be firmly placed 'out there', away from you, in the public arena. Traditionally a lot of women's work has been invisible, tending to other people's lives, and the only real testament of value has been the achievements of others. That 'invisible' work, such an integral part of parenting, needs to be valued by both parents, and seen to be as significant as any achievement 'out there' in the world.

Many of the great heroes of this century, such as Albert Einstein and Winston Churchill, failed appallingly in terms of their responsibilities to their families. When we talk about success we talk about it in terms of people's work and what they achieved for mankind, but it's always easier to achieve very highly in one sphere if you don't really have to concentrate on others. If we think in terms of being successful across the board, in work, in one-to-one relationships, in our families, in our communities, then a much more searching and complex notion of success is created. Some years ago, I attended a friend's father's funeral, a man esteemed in his professional capacity. Amidst the pomp and ceremony of the funeral, which primarily celebrated the man's work achievement, I thought of how cold and distant his children had found him and how insignificant they had felt to him. If we could come back to the personal and claim the value of human relationships, now that would be progress.

Quite often, I've been at talks or seminars where some expert on children, education or childcare was speaking. If you assess that person's schedule, they can't possibly be spending much time with their own children. Does this make sense? It is time to look for the discrepancies in our lives and rectify them. As one teenager said to me in speaking about her mother, an ardent campaigner and innovator, 'She was everyone's mother, but she wasn't there when we needed her'. Public acclaim is wonderful, but sticking with the commitment to our own children in an ongoing, often unseen, steady manner is what is required. Hearing their problems, seeing them through difficulties; this is what will build and strengthen our future society. It's amazing how many books are written on family life, family dynamics and teenager's problems by men who rarely, if ever, spend long hours day after day with their children or by men who do not have or live with children. I have had the experience of being part of a couple without children, of having children and being away from them for long hours of working, and of consistently and regularly spending long hours with them while also maintaining a career. I'm convinced that the prolonged hours day after day give the most realistic view of just how difficult child raising is. The amount a parent has to deal with if there is more than one child is colossal, yet being there in an ongoing regular manner will help them to know and understand themselves in a profound way. You as a parent will also know your children and not some manufactured illusion of them.

Sometimes people, particularly women, who normally carry the burden of childcare are overwhelmed by the amount of demands in their lives. The breaking point may be that they concede on something which is really important to their lives, like a course or an interest they've taken up. Women are very good at supporting and facilitating others to fulfil their dreams – look at all the women still who row in behind high-achieving partners. We are fortunate in Ireland in that we've had two female presidents whose partners have done likewise. Equality would ensure that both partners pursue their dreams, but not to the deficit of the children receiving support for the life stages they are encountering. If the women referred to above had asked for support from their partner, sought assistance elsewhere, or engaged in some creative brain-storming, it mightn't have been necessary to capitulate on things they'd struggled to obtain or achieve. Resentment creeps in before long, and it feels like everyone gets their priorities responded to except you. This leads to the martyrdom syndrome, which has nothing to do with assessing matters and making mature decisions. If there's a martyr in the house, everyone pays a price.

A holistic, integrated way of living as a family means that everyone has rights and needs which ought to be respected. I've met numerous children who are continually uprooted and asked to move school, change friends, sometimes take on a different culture and language, because of the job of one parent. Such children find it hard to settle in one place as they know they'll be moving again in two or three years. Parents are often oblivious to the difficulties for the children, because of course they do adapt. In such situations, frequently one person's career has the priority with the other person's work seen as secondary, something which can be let go of if necessary. An integrated approach would be for the employments of both parents to be respected alongside the needs/preferences of the children, and then decisions taken jointly within that framework. Anyone who has ever tried making joint decisions will identify how difficult it is to do, and how much easier it is to make decisions alone. If joint decision-making proves difficult, it is easy to imagine how difficult it is to work towards group decisions. I worked in a feminist collective for a number of years where all decisions were made by consensus. It was a long, tedious and frustrating experience, which nevertheless proved to be invaluable later in being a parent and facilitating collective decision-making procedures. You need to believe strongly in such a procedure, otherwise you will lose your nerve at a crucial point and interfere, thus scuttling the process. Operating such strategies ensures that everyone gets what they want, but in lesser quantities. If children were to experience this kind of decision-making in their families and in schools, it would be a solid preparation for taking responsibility in adult life and for decision-making as part of a company or other grouping. It would place the issues of respect and relationship solidly in the context of human dynamics. It becomes harder to disregard someone or his needs when there is a relationship established – issues of fairness and justice have a stronger footing. Instead, what children and teenagers learn is that adults pay lip service to respecting their rights and then go right on and do as they choose.

Many schools include assertiveness training in their Transition Year Programmes, yet when those pupils try to put something of what they've learned into operation in their schools, they are bossed and bullied and told what to do. These teenagers are aged sixteen and seventeen, soon to be out in the world, and this is how they are treated in an educational system which is supposedly about preparing them to take their place in the world. Teenagers are rebelling against such treatment and schools such as the 'grind schools', which the teacher's organisations do not favour, are becoming more popular. Such schools are treated as a business where the client must be satisfied. While I disagree with the cramming nature of their approach to education, and feel there are many things they do not offer, it is also clear that they realise young people must be respected and are aiming to do just that in their treatment of them.

Most of the self-help literature suggests that all you have to do is identify what you clearly want and go for it. It takes little or no account of what happens in people's lives when they attempt to do this, apart from the instructions about combating 'negative thought patterns' with daily positive affirmations!

Human beings are complex, with complex emotional lives and thought patterns. To be afforded the possibility of changing the direction of your life and mapping out the life you want, instead of the one that seems to befall you, is innovative and wonderful. Most of the self-help literature speaks of leaving behind negative thought patterns and downward spirals, moving toward the light. However, in bringing your life into focus and working positively on your actions, thoughts and emotions, and in achieving perhaps lots of things that you always wanted to, you will also be invoking the 'shadow' aspects of yourself. These are aspects of yourself that are very unintegrated and have been unexpressed in your life so far, but which have a strength and force within them which you may not be prepared for or able to cope with. If understood and anticipated, this energy might not develop into destructiveness as it sometimes does. I've seen people turn on themselves in a ferocious manner, swiping away months or years of progress. Moving into a positive frame of mind, and working with a new paradigm of being in charge and able to choose, is best achieved by slow, prepared steps where support structures are enlisted over a long period of time. To commence such major renovation on your personality, scaffolding needs to be put in place to support this refurbishment, otherwise the house may not withstand such changes. But who tells you this? Crashing through old binding behaviours unleashes destructive energies which must be managed. Everyone knows that people need support when they are having a hard time, but few realise that people need even greater support when they are progressing through difficulties and changing their lives. Without that sustained support, and the understanding of what may occur, people can be only too willing to blame themselves for having done something wrong.

The 'having it all' idea or positive thinking is not a simple process; one's innermost core beliefs are being unearthed and challenged. A person can be brought to the edge of a nervous breakdown or indeed fully into it. Caution and self-care must be the primary factors and baby steps are much more lasting. I'm not suggesting that people ought not to strive to change the direction of their life or address the 'stuckness' or boredom they experience. I do support innovations and changes, but at a steady, sustainable pace. Changing the way you feel, think or operate is wonderful but direction should be sought and resistances taken account of. Ask what the old patterns were holding in place, and you'll begin to see that as you remove more and more limitations from your life, greater and greater responsibilities must be undertaken. I've seen many examples of people consumed by their own progress who race on, giving themselves more and more, while concurrently becoming more and more blind to the needs of those around them. The 'having it all' ideal means just that. You will 'have it all' or at least more of yourself, but maybe more than you bargained for. In pursuing the 'all' you will encounter more of yourself; are you prepared for that? Evoking the positive in yourself is a fine ideal, as long as you are aware that you will evoke the same strength of negativity – there will be a matching of energies which requires serious attention to manage and negotiate your way through.

Principles of maturity don't seem to get activated spontaneously within this process. If people have lived deprived, restricted or limited lives they may never have had to encounter such moral choices. Now is the time to learn what's right within the morality of choice, not simply what you can have or do. If key transitional experiences have been missed out on it may be difficult to resist the pull to give them to yourself now. Some therapies or theories talk about recouping as if you can simply furnish yourself now with experiences from the past. It is important to remember the life stage you are at, and that actions /decisions need to be incorporated smoothly into that. Encouraging a sense of integrity within the self needs to accompany such actions. Integrity means being able to see beyond your own needs and attempting some understanding of others. Greater peace and happiness will be achieved if decisions are built on this basis. The idea of the 'pain of happiness' is a dysfunctional and futile notion; if you are feeling this it is usually because your happiness is built on the unhappiness or misery of others associated with you.

Of course, the way one approaches such changes can help

or hinder. Sometimes people bring in a fervent religious-like zeal which has little to do with openness to change or possibilities and much to do with compulsive control. The 'having it all' then becomes a punishing schedule of adherence to certain beliefs, activities and mantras after which one will be duly rewarded. In terms of morality, many actions cannot be clearly defined as right or wrong but the 'rightness' or 'wrongness' exists in how the action or activity is undertaken. Someone trapped in a compulsive way of being can convert the best of intentions into something bad. If the basis for action is fear and low self-esteem, then clearly the person is trying to convert himself/herself to an acceptable/loved/successful human being. But it will never happen unless those underlying feelings are accepted and a sympathy and warmth is engendered towards the self. This is not something that can be pushed, rushed or manufactured. People can be damaged by their upbringing. If the deficits are great then you may be seriously disadvantaged. That is not your fault. Seek out your talents, accept your shortcomings and befriend yourself, but not in the phoney, defensive, illusion-ridden manner that so often is encouraged. To move from a position of low self-esteem to an inflated ego is not progress, it is mere delusion.

We have made 'success', that outward statement which is evidence that we've done well, our god and dictator. Success looks like a high income, a house in a good area, cars and various other paraphernalia, being invited to the right events, thus being acknowledged by others as successful. It is irrelevant if you are causing yourself physical ill-health or psychological manicness which you then have to spend money, time and energy trying to alleviate. Similar scenarios exist about sports; people overwork, then they need time to play their sports in order to unwind, instead of being home. It is seen to be irrelevant if children are spending more and more time out of the sphere of parental care. They are being sent to good schools, on foreign holidays and summer camps, and enjoy all of the trappings of wealth earned diligently by their hard-living, hard-working parents. Therefore everything is alright – we are getting there, wherever that is! The assumption is that the neglected children will be affirming of the parent's actions, perhaps even grateful.

The whole concept of career success needs continually to be evaluated. For many people, too much is invested in their work and if that changes or people are requested to accept early retirement, devastation follows. We can no longer achieve a success in one area of our life and feel we'll be pardoned for all the other failings. Working hours need to diminish to make way for all the other aspects of life which we need to succeed in; a career will be perhaps only one aspect of work that you do. On the positive side, if we can move towards this we will achieve a more integrated, happy and fulfilling life. Work may change as we do, but if so, it will bring with it the capacity to offer much more in terms of human growth and potential for the individual. The idea of 'having it all' is often set up as something that is clearly recognisable, a sort of list where one can tick off each item. But when you see the list of projects people are involved in, as well as having children they are responsible for, a simple calculation of hours will tell you that:

a) they are not spending much time with their children, and

b) they spend very little time alone.

If we are fully in our lives and living them well, not very much about that life may seem extraordinary; as Carol Orsborn says, 'When you are living life fully, you are not doing things you think of as great. You merely do what's next.'

In the past I've experienced a distance from my life. I've looked at it and was impressed. But it was also really difficult at that time to keep hold of my life as I was dragged hither and thither by so many demands. The 'having it all' idea contributes to the idea of 'no limits'; people are often encouraged to believe that they have no limitations or at least ought not to experience them, that there are no limits to what they can have, do, be and so on. While there is little doubt that most people actually utilise very little of their abilities and benefit greatly from endeavours to widen their horizons, there is also a purpose to limitations – we are actively psychologically contained by them. Rollo May the philosopher says, 'Devoid of limitation, we'd be like a river without banks'. The Jungian idea of containment suggests that people are held, in a positive sense, by many things in their lives. These things can be routine activities, regular events, style of living, even the way that one presents oneself in society. If people change many things about themselves radically, that will have a psychological impact that they need to anticipate, otherwise they may go on to spend years shoring up difficulties without any real progress being made.

'Famous' has become indistinguishable from 'successful', and what has become synonymous with success so often is plainly daft. It is time to begin to offer alternative notions of success, to honour people for the good they do but only if it is in the overall context of their lives. Within this framework the heights of artistic talent, sometimes bought through the sacrifice of others, may not be worthy of the same acclaim. People are deemed to have reached the higher echelons of success when they've acquired status and usually monetary reward. However, status is an amorphous concept touching quite close at times to the notorious, and even farcical, and may have little to do with providing the universe with anything useful or worthwhile. Generosity equally receives high acclaim; individuals and corporations who make hefty donations to charity are lauded. It is always worth considering how the money was obtained in the first place; were workers exploited, was fairness upheld, were people duped?

Carol Orsborn, in her book *Inner Excellence at Work*, talks of life-driven work as being very different to manicness. 'In order to find a lasting experience of success, you must learn to tap into new, life-driven sources of inspiration, creativity and vitality.' Both she and Covey feel that people can expend considerable energy and effort in thwarting their efforts to succeed, if the source is not in keeping with the values of the person. But people can also expend energy thwarting their efforts from another perspective, lack of confidence and dislike of self. She gives the example of her own life, which was manic and driven; she and her partner pulled back, whittled things down, created a more balanced, all-round existence and then found, to their astonishment, that their income and profits were up. Covey, in *The Seven Habits of Highly Effective People*, quotes numerous examples when businesses or employers considered issues such as the other person, integrity, honesty and so on, and the result was that solutions were found to problems much faster and productivity rose. However, he is quick to point out that it cannot simply be a strategy or a 'cosmetic job'; the people involved must be genuinely committed to what they are trying to achieve. It's about trying to work from the heart and the principled part of the self. To locate a job that is enhancing to you, and those around you, is a wonderful thing; if all elements are in keeping with your own heart then it will be almost impossible for that not to be reflected in a worthy life, including financial gains (but probably not excessive wealth). However, it's fair to say that some people truly seem to have an ingenuity in turning dust to gold and if it is not harming the individual, or those associated with the project, and can be distributed or shared, then it may well be a valuable engagement of talents.

Attempting to create a more integrated life is the task of this new century. Men and women agree that it is really difficult, and sometimes near impossible, for a partnership to keep both careers advancing, earn a sufficient amount to meet the demands of family life, have both parents spending considerable time with children each week, sharing in domestic chores and maintaining a relationship with each other which is dynamic, challenging and growthful for each person. I suggest it is possible to achieve three-quarters of this, once you concede to letting part of it go, but achieving it all is what we need to be aiming for and what is most profoundly difficult. Speaking with peers and observing situations, it becomes clearer just how difficult. Couples who don't have children and have careers long term will often manage their relationship very successfully.

Others will manage careers and children successfully but opt for multiple adult relationships. Traditional relationships may succeed because the roles are defined but individual needs are subsumed. In relationships where both parents work outside the home, often the shortfall is in how the children are cared for. Likewise, people may create a harmonious homelife to the detriment of their working life; they are unfair to employers, take frequent days off and generally do not seek excellence in their work. But for parents who attempt to include joint parenting and joint earning, whilst maintaining a successful relationship and parenting capably, the pressures are great, sometimes overwhelming. The 'having it all' in this context is about growing up, being mature, accepting responsibilities and really endeavouring to do the best for others as well as yourself. Seeking to bring forth the best in yourself in the combination of all these efforts will bring about true personal growth.

Finally, it is also true that people can and do make the same mistakes and create the same life for themselves over and over again, living out a 'self-fulfilling prophecy'. It is tragic that people who've had very difficult childhoods frequently go on to choose lovers, jobs, living circumstances which in turn offer them little love or comfort. To turn such programming around takes a lot of patience, determination and skill and will not be achieved easily; it may be a life-long task. But of course every positive step is a building of character and hope on which to build further and is certainly worthwhile. People do succeed in 'having it all', in terms of learning to choose wisely for themselves, assessing how they live their lives, taking responsibility for their mistakes and difficulties and not blaming others. The greater the capacity we create within ourselves for joy, acceptance and trust in the positive forces of life, the more possibilities we open ourselves to.

One really interesting way to think of your life is in terms of what you'd have to say about it if you were going to die tomorrow. Where do you feel you've failed yourself, where have you not fulfilled dreams, where have you been lacking courage in your choices? Where do you feel you've already missed the boat, and what can you do about that to give yourself a second chance? It's amazing how the idea of death helps to focus the mind. The unfortunate thing is that far too often we live our lives as if we have endless choices and no expiry date. Then when/if we are faced with the prospect of death, there is perhaps little time to assess our choices or change matters.

Chapter 10

SOLUTIONS

The traditional viewpoint has been that women should be the primary caretaker. The beliefs supporting this stance usually are that women are better at it, that they have a greater life training, ability and desire for the task, and that children need and benefit more from constancy of attention from the mother. This position requires that the man take the 'provider' role. Our problem in Ireland is that while things are changing at a breathtaking pace in terms of the number of women working outside the home, and the constant focus on the father's necessity to become an intimate and constant parent in his children's lives, there is still a glorification of the mother who is seen to sacrifice all in remaining at home to care for her children. This sort of thinking is leftover debris from the syndrome of the Irish 'mammy', the woman who, in the midst of financial struggle, emotional strife, and probably very little assistance from her husband, provided admirably for her family, materially and emotionally. Very often she motivated her family, particularly her sons, to do well in life, and they remained in such awe of her inordinate struggle and sacrifice that they were never quite able to leave her. Nobody would ever match up to that icon.

The reality is that just as the structure and ethos of Irish families are changing and women and men's role are digressing from the traditional, the centrality of the position of the mother in the Irish family must change too. Men must be allowed to cohabit that inner sanctum, that central position, with women.

Men are being asked to concede in the area of work, so women must do likewise in the family. Men are being challenged to shift their work out of the central place it has occupied for so long in their hearts and minds and make space for their families so women must let go of the control they've exerted within the domestic arena. Traditionally men have been used to observing the intimacy of their wife with the children from the sidelines. Women now berate them for not being more involved in the emotional and domestic life of the family, and yet they are uneasy about conceding that central position and abandoning the stance of relationship expert in the family. Research has shown that men who've been part of peer coupleships have a very different experience from traditional fathers about the role the children play in the couple's emotional life. They are seen neither as separate nor as any kind of threat to the emotional life of the couple by peer fathers, whereas the traditional father sees them as having a very strong bond with their mother, sometimes to his exclusion. This he accepts, since he has a different role, and he doesn't seek to involve himself in the everyday intimacies which successfully build a strong rapport. He accepts this as a fait accompli, which perpetuates the myth that women are naturally closer to their children than men and vice versa. Just look at family situations where the father is left as the sole carer, and how successfully a very close, intimate bond is developed; such fathers sometimes admit this would not exist if the mother was still in the picture.

A further dilemma often emerges in the form of the husband's job prospects or income. Because men frequently have the capacity of earning more than women, the husband's job can be given priority, or concessions made to facilitate him in a subtle or less obvious manner. Women have become used to letting go of promotions and status in favour of their family commitments. Men must begin to do similarly – the couple must make the best attempt they can to create a wholesome family life, and that means that the family must be the priority, not money, status or promotion prospects. Couples become equal partners not just by chance; they must work hard long-term to avoid the pitfalls that exist. They must be creative in their choices, remaining constantly open to new possibilities. If men and women can hold firm in that commitment, work situations will be forced to adapt. Businesses which don't will end up with only a young, inexperienced workforce, since parents will seek alternative job circumstances or become self-employed.

It's about knowing what you want, and sometimes that only becomes clear as you engage in something. Agreeing to an arrangement can seem fine in theory, but sometimes the practice of it is a very different experience. I've met with many men who were deeply hurt by their wives' rejection of the traditional role and thereby, in their eyes, what they had given them. The wives in turn, felt it had taken them years to realise the arrangement wasn't working and now an array of factors within it, and aspects of it, constituted many of their grievances. Blame and recriminations usually lead nowhere except into righteousness and blindness. If you are realising that things aren't functioning in the most productive and caring manner in your life, it simply means it's time to change things. Don't waste time and energy getting stuck in anger and castigation. Stephen Covey speaks of being 'proactive', i.e. taking an action that will improve the situation, not disimprove it. It's really the only solution. But patience, action and strength are required, and you may have to input extensively for a protracted period without seeing much of a result. It's a bit like renovating a house; a lot of upheaval and dismantling has to occur, and for a time, it looks:

a) worse than it ever did, and

b) like it will never come together.

Then suddenly when all the solid, strengthening work is complete, the decoration is done and it's finished. Begin with even vague notions of what you want to change, whether it is aspects of the couple's relationship, domestic arrangements or childcare options, and get working on that. This is the project that requires your energy and effort – don't squander your resources on the past. If you wish to begin by assessing the overall system that you're operating within and part of, include all of the factors and that may help give you a clearer perspective on what is working well and what needs to be modified. Just remember that things are not changed overnight.

You don't get from A-Z without going through a lot of other steps in between. While it is crucial to know clearly where you want to get to, the steps in between must also be clearly mapped out. You must be committed to finding a solution. People often give up before investigating all the possibilities because they are not really determined enough. The first thing is to look carefully at your family life, draw it out on a large sheet, list each member, and where each person is capable of vocalising their needs and ask them what they are happy and not happy with. If one or more members are babies and incapable of speaking for themselves, look at the issues in this book and try to answer honestly what you think. Ask other members of your extended family, such as the grandparents of the children or aunts/uncles, what they think about the children's lives. There are always a lot of varied opinions in a family, some of which may be very useful to include in your thinking, but do not ask if you are simply going to be defensive and sullen if their view of your family life doesn't match yours. It is really courageous of people to tell you what they think if they know beforehand that the viewpoints will conflict. Parents are sometimes so lacking in confidence in their parenting and childcare choices that they are afraid to ask others' opinions for fear they will lose further confidence. Try to remember that you are making crucial decisions about your children's lives and therefore it's worthwhile putting up with a little unease if ultimately it helps you to make wiser and more informed choices.

Ensure that you have sufficient information, seek out what you don't understand or need further information on. Speak to people, friends, colleagues and relatives. Include all of this on your sheet. Having encompassed what each of the parents want, being as specific and as inclusive as you can, now look at the overall needs listed. Remember this is a piece of work that may take weeks or months to complete, and further time to actually realise. Don't leap to seeking the solutions until you are clear what the problems are. If you move too fast towards seeking the solution, you may err on the side of not being inclusive enough. Also, and more importantly, each step will slowly progress you toward the next so if you don't go through them all, you won't have released the resources for the final decisions.

When you have the full picture laid out in front of you, begin to prioritise; if you are a lone parent seek assistance from another adult at this point, and if there are two parents then sit down when you are assured of uninterrupted time and look at the picture. For example, it might look something like this:

Parent A	*Parent B*	*Child/female Aged 4*	*Child/male Aged 8*
Time working	Time working	Time in school	Time in school
Time at home	Time at home	Time with minder	Time with minder
Breakdown of time at home	Breakdown of time at home	Babysitting at weekends	Babysitting at weekends
Time socialising	Time socialising	Other activities	Other activities
Responsibility for chores?	Responsibility for chores?		
Time as a couple together	Time as a couple together		

- How much time does each parent spend with children?
- How much time do children spend being minded?
- Who gets them up in the mornings?
- Who puts them to bed?
- Who does the homework?
- How much time are children with other adults?
- Who brings them to school?
- Who collects them?

• Name all the specific tasks to do with the children and the home.

Seeing something written down brings a clarity; sometimes the reality of the situation only becomes apparent then. People can often maintain illusions about a situation, but when it's written in front of you it's harder to deny.

As a backdrop to these kind of discussions you need to understand what philosophy you're working with; for example, discussions such as who earns most of the income may be relevant if part of the agreement you work with is that the person earning the lesser amount has more to do with the children. So often, parents don't make the 'deal' between them explicit and then get upset when the other partner looks for something more or doesn't keep their side of the bargain. Be as clear and as specific as possible in your needs and your requirements, both in terms of what you are agreeing to and what you wish to change. Remember also that couples have the most arguments about childminding and domestic issues.

Then go to the desired situation, for example:

Parent A	*Parent B*	*Child A*	*Child B*
Wants to work more but could work from home perhaps in evenings Want to take up a hobby Wants to socialise more	Wants to work less Wants to do further study Wants more time with children	Wants less time with minder Wants to have friends to home at weekends	Wants to be collected from school Wants family activities at the weekends

Given the amount of time in the week, a reality check may need to be installed in terms of all that is requested and a longer view taken. Perhaps things that can't be included in the weekly schedule could be considered for holiday periods, such as hobbies or extra time with friends. But that needs to be agreed on now as discussions of holidays may cause further problems. Remember the basis of all problems is a lack of, or an inability to communicate. If you and your partner don't have those skills then you need to learn them as no progress can be made if every attempt to communicate is going to flounder in an emotional abyss of blame and recrimination. It's like trying to make a cake without having first sought out the ingredients. In my experience, it is the healthiest and most resourceful couples who disagree and then put effort into finding solutions to their problems. The relationship that is problem-free or argument-free is probably not very deep or challenging. Couples sometimes strike an unconscious 'deal' with each other – I won't upset you and you, in return, won't upset me. Such coupleships do not provide a forum for growth. They will remain accomodating but superficial. Arguments or differences are not to be feared but remember skills are required to facilitate the passage through such arguments and disagreements. Solutions must ultimately be mutually agreed. Wild gratuitous rows will not encourage that, they merely let off steam.

Predominantly, people enter and commit to long-term relationships in the unconscious hope and desire of resolving childhood conflicts and getting needs, which still remain unmet, taken care of. This is not as catastrophic a beginning as it sounds if the couple can utilise the coupleship as an arena for growing up and developing mature adult responses. If, however, each partner remains inflexibly petulant and stubborn then they can become locked into a pattern of behaviour, a reaction and counter-reaction cycle which remains repetitive and stuck. This cycle leaves very little space for developing resources for dealing with life's crises or difficulties, individual personal queries or questions and an almost complete depletion of resources for conflictual interpersonal dialogue. People are not learning sufficient skills in emotional literacy as children at home or in school but a further opportunity exists for people to grow up in their adult coupleships. Destructive cycles must be broken, adults cannot continue to behave defensively and immaturely and hope to parent well or to be a good partner. The collusive patterns of behaviour which couples set up between them ensuring that a blindness will exist in their treatment of their children must be loosened and let go of. All of this will only incur if people will take the time to learn the tools of interpersonal dialogue and commit to personal growth and change instead of remaining isolated and frightened, working from a meagre repertoire of responses developed much earlier in life, usually having as an aim the protection of a fragile psychological self.

There are four ingredients to seeking solutions or addressing difficulties within the context of working with process. They are:

1. Intention.

2. Preliminary arrangements – setting in motion.

3. Action – which will have an impact and bring about change.

4. Facing/staying with/processing consequences.

If you follow these steps, moving only from one to the other when you're ready, but doing as much as you can associated with the step you're working on, and not stopping then you allow yourself to see and understand matters in a way you might not otherwise have had the opportunity to do, while at the same time moving towards your goal.

In an earlier chapter I spoke about Irish men leaving relationships quite suddenly – the experience of desertion for the female partner. Men do not like dealing with the complex and messy emotions pertaining to a break-up. They may not have the emotional maturity to deal with problems within the relationship and see the only option is to leave but then neither can they bear the difficulty of dealing with that – hence desertion. The problem with this kind of resolution is that ultimately nothing has really been sorted out. If one continues to run from problems then the opportunity to grow from those situations and difficulties is also dismissed perhaps even the opportunity to 'grow up' is usurped. The person abandoning ship in such a circumstance is opting for a comfort zone of 'no conflict'. This is not a realistic expectation of life, unless one is going to live ostrich-style, head in the sand, avoiding any conflictual situations as many people try to do. Of course that doesn't ultimately work either as those same difficulties frequently follow you to the next relationship. It's always better to deal with things and work them out slowly with the exception of situations of violence or threat, then crises intervention is required, since the circumstances are critical and perhaps life-threatening. If you can't face something in a relationship, and the difficulty is often stated as something the other person is doing, such as bullying you, not listening to you, not understanding you, attempt to really face and deal with that and then decide if you still wish to depart. The ingredients within successful resolutions are:

a) Do not ignore what you are feeling or if you are concerned/unhappy about something – it will not go away by ignoring it;

b) After reflection, speak to your partner in a reasonable manner, not when you are angry or have taken alcohol. (The 'great' conversations which take place when alcohol has been consumed rarely form the foundation for solving anything);

c) State fully, but as succinctly as you can, what the problems are for you. Do not blame or demand agreement. Speak about how you understand the situation, what you feel upset about, and any ideas you have for a resolution;

d) Be prepared to listen to what the other person has to say;

e) Finally, and most importantly, agree on a time to speak about this issue again. Even if a solution has been found and agreed upon, it is still important to make this arrangement in order to see if the solution is being executed or if it is working. So often, couples complete all of these steps but omit the final one and so the best-made plan flounders. It can be really difficult to muster the energy, find the time, or have the interest, to pursue the matter further until it becomes critical again. Then the solution is required immediately and that causes further problems because every discussion is anxiety-filled and urgent.

Historically, women are frequently seen as the relationship expert in the coupleship and are the instigators of such conversations. Men need to begin to initiate such discussions; it is part and parcel of taking responsibility within the life of the family. Men tell me they fear such conversations, feel too much is being asked of them and frequently take a position of resistance, hoping the problem will disappear if too much isn't made of it. They believe that women frequently make 'too much' of things, in other words have strong reactions about things which they, the men, don't perceive to be that important. Dialogue would of course help, as Deborah Tannen shows in *You Just Don't Understand*, women sometimes are satisfied that simply the conversation has taken place even if major resolutions are not the outcome. It satisfies their need for communication and offers reassurance about the caring nature of the relationship.

Another important concept to consider when looking at the life of your family is when is enough enough. What do you consider enough? While everyone agrees that income must correspond to outgoings it is important to consider what is enough in financial terms. As human beings we have a desire to progress, that usually means achieving more in the work environment, becoming better known, earning more, moving to a larger house and so on. There is nothing problematic about these aspirations so long as they don't interfere with the overall balance of your life in terms of time for your children, and your primary relationship. It is not really rational to simply want more and more purely for 'the more'. After achieving a certain level of financial ease, and comfort in living, accumulating more and more is not really going to make much of a difference to your quality of life but the effort required may create a huge deficit in terms of the time available for those you love. Being famous in the world of celebrities illustrates perfectly what I mean. You must keep yourself in public view in terms of appearances, activities and achievements, otherwise people forget about you and you slide into anonymity. So, it is important for you yourself to be capable of assessing and deciding when enough is enough, otherwise you are doomed to continue on a tyrannising treadmill which ultimately leaves you feeling empty and compromised at the end of your life. In so many ways, and in so many aspects of your life with your family, things are fleeting; the time to spend evenings with your two year old will not come again, the chats with your seven year old may not occur when he's eight and so on. In terms of building rapport with your children, occasions come and go and that is that. If you continue to neglect such opportunities it is at the peril of damaging that relationship, and thereby missing the opportunity to enter that rich world of intimacy. The film 'One True Thing', in which Meryll Streep stars as the mother dying of cancer who has spent a lifetime engaged in that 'invisible work' of parenting spoken of earlier in the book, illustrates that the most complete test of your life is whether or not you've loved and respected those put into your care. Have you dared to open your heart to loving them in the fullest manner which will, in turn, ensure that you are no longer capable of being negligent?

As Irish people we've always had to struggle against something; against poverty, against oppression, against suppression of our religion, against being denied an education so it is part of our own psyche. We still engage strongly with the idea of the existence of some adversary to struggle against; it may be the community/family who'll be surprised to see you doing so well, it may be the teachers who never saw you as being particularly bright, it may be the society which treated your parents badly. If engaged in such a process it becomes more or less impossible to determine when enough is enough because the goalposts continue to move.

The single-mindedness which people often bring to bear on their life is not the answer. Being multi-focused is what is required. Being multi-skilled and constantly open to acquiring new skills and furnishing yourself with greater and greater abilities for your life as you get older. Growing up doesn't just get completed by the twenties and that's it. You're now equipped for life. Equally, you don't simply form a relationship and have children, have a few hard years and now you're an expert. At each stage in your life, different skills are required, they are event-related. Then also each decade of your life requires you to be in a different kind of engagement with life's process. Different aspects of the self must be called forth in the fifties than in the thirties. To continue to engage in life's process interminably one is required to grow in terms of keeping all of the focuses of your life in view. Being single-minded is easy in comparison, and in essence it's a cop-out of all the conflicting difficulties encountered when one tries to manage it all. The advantage, and you'll be happy to know there is an advantage, of trying to manage it all, is that there are linkages between everything; everything in our lives is in fact connected. Solutions to life's dilemmas are not always found in the specific area to which they relate. Sometimes an understanding can emerge from a most unexpected source once you embrace the notion of everything being connected. Synchronicity, the idea coined by Carl Jung, to explain how the meaningful coincidences of events which are causally unrelated can evoke palpable revelations of consciousness once one is prepared to be open to the phenomenon.

Very often, as stated in earlier chapters, people start something with great enthusiasm and then hampering difficulties, which are not negotiated, arise. Sometimes people do very well in their parenting in the more difficult years of babyhood and then fare quite badly in their efforts when the children are teenagers. Constant awareness of the skills required must be maintained, alongside constant monitoring and discussion of how you're doing. Working as a psychotherapist, it was amazing sometimes to observe the differences in how different members of a family had been parented. Clearly nothing stands still. So many factors impact on how well the couple is parenting, particularly the marital relationship, and matters can disimprove incredibly, sometimes over a relatively short period of time. Parents need to be supported to parent well, to be capable of seeing their children's difficulties and needs and to find the energy, emotional rapport and time to respond to them. But if parents, as the leaders of that family, can manage to mediate difficulties then everything runs more smoothly. Difficulties don't need to become crises, issues remain resolvable and children witness parents coping well with their lives, being fair and compassionate to them as children, and committed in their adult intimate relationship. The amount of learning that children do within such an environment is profound. They are acquiring skills daily which will launch them into adulthood as loving, capable human beings. What parents wouldn't want that for their children? And yet so frequently we thwart their learning because we lack courage to face our own inadequacies and address them.

Parenting children in many regards is still seen as a background occupation, something you do behind all the other important things you do in your life 'out there'. If people have true self-esteem and value themselves they are able to see the importance of parenting, what it takes for people to do it well, the positive impacts it would have on our future society and future generations in your own family line, and the sense of satisfaction and completeness it engenders. Parenting is never finished no matter how old the 'child' is. People talk frequently of wanting to do something with their life, something life-changing, significant, profound. How about doing it, daily, with your children? It may not bring you laurels or make you a Nobel Prize winner but it will, if you allow, challenge you more than perhaps anything else in your life.

Parents ought to clearly question themselves on how they are parenting and install some procedures of support, assessment and accountability, thereby assisting themselves to do the very best they can. Being a good parent one year doesn't mean you'll be that the following one. There is nothing that can be taken for granted about parenting well. Parents must remain on a constant learning curve.

Just think for a moment of your career, think of the training you've received, how you must keep yourself up to date on new thinking within that field, how you assess your performance or as assessed, offered feedback and challenges, assisted by colleagues and how much all of that helps you to perform at your peak and grow as a person. Now think of yourself as a parent. What support do you receive? How do you assess yourself? Where are you accountable? Do yourself and your partner talk about your children in terms of how they are coping in their lives, do you give each other feedback on how you are parenting? Frequently people feel defensive about this, and think that parenting comes naturally and one shouldn't analyse the skills therein for fear of losing them or disrupting the naturalness of parenting. Yet most people learn how to parent from how they've been parented and most are critical of the type of parenting they received. So, are most people then operating as parents with little information and meagre skills? It would seem so, mainly because of the lack of existing forums to discuss aspects of parenting one is concerned about, apart from the arena of psychotherapy which a lot of people would be unwilling to enter.

I suggest it is time to think of relationship and parental coaching as something that is necessary for every couple and parent, due to the sort of life we lead today. Do not confuse this with therapy; it is similar to the idea of a life coach. Couples could assess how they are doing, specific recommendations may be offered such as entering psychotherapy or counselling if deemed necessary, taking classes in communication skills, creating a forum to speak of their sexual relationship or financial issues or any other aspect of the relationship which appears to be causing problems. The important thing about coaching is that that is precisely what it is. It's not about sitting down and going through problems. That has to be done elsewhere, it's not about anyone else finding solutions. It's about the couple being active in finding their own resources and not opting out. If you decide to use coaching I suggest you meet with the coach no more than four times a year and that you work hard in between those times to achieve your goals. If you are not progressing then options of assistance can be offered in between those assessment times while still adhering to returning for the coaching session every three or four months in order to establish levels of satisfaction with progress and with your life in general. Obviously, something like coaching cannot deal with lives where trauma and severe loss has occurred, nor can it deal with people who wish to offer themselves opportunities to explore their inner thoughts and motivations. Nevertheless, it is a valuable tool and should perhaps be included in the modern schemata of parenting.

Solutions lie in valuing the ordinary aspects of life and cultivating the ability to see them as extraordinary in their ordinariness, treating ourselves, our children and others well, valuing what we have and daily giving thanks and celebrating it, and retaining our sensitivity to our dreams and possibilities. From that basis and in that manner, to progress our lives will not be difficult or harsh. Driving ambition and seeking our fortune compulsively merely adds to a never-ending search for something, which can never be met in that way. All of us wish to experience a sense of connection with others and the validness of our own existence. Working hard, doing well in your job, achieving your goals, and pursuing your dreams are all possible once you bear in mind that life and living is encompassed in the pursuit, not in the arrival at the set goal. Life is in the living. Do not usurp the opportunities in your life to experience a loving and wholesome existence.

AFTERWORD

In Budget 2001 there was a progression from the previous budget and, as anticipated, there was an increase in the allocation of funds to childcare. We are going in the right direction, for sure, but are these things sufficient to ease the seriousness of existing difficulties surrounding the whole childcare issue? Child benefit was increased by more than 50% but childcare costs are still not eligible for tax relief which means that parents paying increasingly exorbitant childcare fees will experience little real relief from the financial burden they are straining under.

However, there was evidence of the commitment to improve crèche and childcare facilities in the following:

• Capital grants were made available for commercial crèches and community-based childcare facilities.
• Staff grants for community-based projects were made available.
• Childcare employment grants will be available.
• Provision of childcare in local authority developments.
• National childminders initiative.
• National after-school initiative.
• Spare classrooms are to be used for childcare.

In keeping with these initiatives the government, as the largest employer in the state, is to set up fifteen Civil Service crèches at a cost of £10 million.

Maternity and adoptive leave is to be extended by four weeks of both paid and unpaid leave. This will ease the stress for mothers anticipating returning to work, especially those breastfeeding, and their babies. Essentially, the longer such leave can be, the better for mother and baby.

APPENDIX

TAKEN FROM THE 'REPORT OF THE PARTNERSHIP 2000 EXPERT WORKING GROUP ON CHILDCARE' (JANUARY 1999)

Summary of reports, legislation, and initiatives in the area of childcare in Ireland between 1980 and 1998 (1)

Name of Body Undertaking Study or Initiative	Date of Publication or Establishment	Appointing Body/Dept.	Summary
Task Force on Childcare Services	1980	Department of Health	Primary focus of Task Force was on the extension and improvement of services for deprived children and children at risk.
Working Party on Childcare Facilities for Working Parents	1982	Department of Labour	Recommended that Department of Health should have overall responsibility for childcare services and an independent National Childcare Authority should be appointed by the Department of Health with representatives from other Government Departments.

Name of Body Undertaking Study or Initiative	Date of Publication or Establishment	Appointing Body/Dept. Summary	
Working Party on Women's Affairs and Family Law Reform	1985	Department of An Taoiseach	Brief was to consider the best administrative measures to promote positive opportunities and facilities to enable women to participate more fully in the life of the community. Recommended a system of registration for childcare facilities based on minimum prescribed standards, an expansion of work-based childcare facilities, making childcare expenses of parents offsetable against income tax.
Committee on Minimum Legal Requirements and Standards for Day Care Services	1985	Department of Health	Recommended introduction of a compulsory registration system of childcare facilities. Also recommended that through the health boards, a new position Area Organiser/co-ordinator for Day Care Services should be established

Name of Body Undertaking Study or Initiative	Date of Publication or Establishment	Appointing Body/Dept.	Summary
			in each Community Care Area to co-ordinate, support and oversee provision of childcare facilities.
National Economic and Social Study on Women's Participation in the Irish Labour Market	1991	NESC	Called for the development of an overall national policy on childcare for working parents – this would be 'the single most important policy to facilitate labour force participation by married women' (Callan & Farrell 1991, pp.8-9).
Report of the Second Commission on the Status of Women	1993	Department of Equality and Law Reform	Considered childcare from the twin perspectives of gender equality in the labour market and child protection and development. Recommendations included: the appointment of childcare co-ordinator in every health board, the

185

Name of Body Undertaking Study or Initiative	Date of Publication or Establishment	Appointing Body/Dept.	Summary
			need for a system to ensure minimally adequate standards in childcare facilities, properly accredited training for all childcare workers and the development of workplace childcare facilities in larger organisations. Department of Equality and Law Reform is responsible for assessing the recommendations of this Commission and drawing up more detailed proposals for action.
Working Group on Childcare Facilities for Working Parents	1994	Department of Equality and Law Reform	Report identified the 'current absence of a national strategy for the general development of childcare provision' and to a lesser extent, 'the fragmentation of responsibility for childcare issues at the level of Government' as the principal reasons for inadequate provision of childcare facilities (Working

Name of Body Undertaking Study or Initiative	Date of Publication or Establishment	Appointing Body/Dept. Summary	
			Group on Childcare Facilities for Working Parents, 1994, pp 3-4).
Evaluation of the Pilot Childcare Initiative	1997	Department of Equality and Law Reform	This initiative (1994-1995) was an initiative of the Department of Equality and Law Reform which involved the expenditure on Childcare of £2.7 million towards the provision of childcare facilities in disadvantaged areas for the purpose of facilitating the participation of socially excluded parents in employment, training or education. The initiative was designed and implemented by the Area Development Management Limited (ADM). The initiative was extended in 1998 with a budgetary allocation of IR£3.6 million p.a. It is now called the Equal Opportunities Childcare Programme.

Name of Body Undertaking Study or Initiative	Date of Publication or Establishment	Appointing Body/Dept.	Summary
United Nations Convention on the Rights of the Child: First National Report of Ireland	1996	Department of Foreign Affairs	The UN Committee on the Rights of the Child is an international body of child rights experts which has been established to monitor the implementation of the Convention. The First National Report of Ireland was submitted by the Irish Government to the UN Committee. Examination of this Report took place during Ireland's plenary session with the UN Committee in Geneva, in January 1998.
Partnership 2000 for Inclusion Employment and Competitiveness	1996	Department of An Taoiseach	Expert Working Group on Childcare was established under the Partnership 2000 agreement, to devise a National Framework for the Development of the Childcare Sector.

Name of Body Undertaking Study or Initiative	Date of Publication or Establishment	Appointing Body/Dept. Summary
Child Care (Pre-School Services) Regulations, Part VII of Child Care Act (1991)	1996	Department of Health — Part VII of the Child Care Act places a statutory duty on health boards to secure the health, safety, and welfare and to promote the development of pre-school children attending pre-school services. The Regulations require adherence to minimum standards with regard to safety, premises, facilities and maintenance of records.
Small Voices: Vital Rights: Submission to the UN Committee on the Rights of the Child by the Children's Rights Alliance	1997	Children's Rights Alliance — The submission represents the views of the Children's Rights Alliance on how Irish law, policy and practice comply with the principles and standards of the Convention and identifies the further measures it considers necessary to ensure compliance.

189

Name of Body Undertaking Study or Initiative	Date of Publication or Establishment	Appointing Body/Dept.	Summary
National Forum for Early Childhood Education	1998	Department of Education and Science	National Forum took place in March 1998. It provided an opportunity for all interested groups to engage in a full exchange of views and for each group to put forward their own particular concerns and objectives towards the development of a national framework for early childhood education. The Report of the National Forum was published in November 1998. A White Paper on Early Education is due to be published by May 1999 which will cover issues such as funding, certification, curriculum and co-ordination.
Equal Opportunities Childcare Programme	1998	Department of Justice, Equality and Law Reform	This programme which is being managed by ADM in conjunction with Department of Justice, Equality and Law Reform contains three funding initiatives: Capital Infrastructure Child-

Name of Body Undertaking Study or Initiative	Date of Publication or Establishment	Appointing Body/Dept. Summary
		care Initiative, Employer Demonstration Childcare Initiative and Community Support Childcare Initiative. All three initiatives are interdependent and strive towards the common aim of improving the quality and quantity of childcare provision in Ireland from an equal opportunities/disadvantaged perspective.
Report of Commission on the family 'Strengthening Families for Life'	1998	Department of Social, Community and Family Affairs	The brief was to examine the needs and priorities of families in the fast-changing social and economic environment. Recommended an approach to supporting families in carrying out their functions which: prioritises investment in the care of young children, supports parents' choices in the care and education of their children, provides practical support and recognition to

Name of Body Undertaking Study or Initiative	Date of Publication or Establishment	Appointing Body/Dept. Summary
		those who undertake the main caring responsibilities for children, facilitates families in balancing work commitments and family life.

BIBLIOGRAPHY

Baker, Robin. (1996) *Sperm Wars: Infidelity, Sexual Conflict and other Bedroom Battles*. London: Fourth Estate.

Baker, Robin and Oram, Elizabeth. (1998) *Baby Wars*. London: Fourth Estate.

Barnardos National Children's Resource Centre and Fingal County Libraries (1998) 'Choosing the Best for Your Child' written by Angela Canavan and Norah Gibbons.

Barnados National Children's Resource Centre. Written and Researched by Maria Dowd (2000) *Get it Right: A Parent's Guide to Choosing Quality Day Care*. Dublin.

_____ (2000) *Check it Out: A Parents Guide to the Pre-School Regulations*. Dublin.

Becker, Ernest. (1973) *The Denial of Death*. New York: Free Press Paperbacks.

Berlin, Isaiah. (1990) *The Crooked Timber of Humanity – Chapters in the History of Ideas*. (John Murray).

Bernard, Jessie. (1973) *The Future of Marriage*. New York: Bantam Books.

Biddulph, Steve. (1991) *More Secrets of Happy Children*. London: Thorsons.

Blumstein, Philip and Schwartz, Pepper. (1983) *American Couples*. New York: William Morrow.

Bly, R. (1990) *Iron John*. Reading, Mass: Addison – Wesley.

Bolles, Richard, Nelson. (1970) *What Colour is Your Parachute?* Berkeley: Ten Speed Press.

Bowers, Fergal. (1994) *Suicide in Ireland*. Dublin: Irish Medical Organisation.

Bowlby, J. (1969, 1973, 1980) *Attachment and Loss*. Vols 1, 2, 3. London: Hogarth Press.

Breggin, Peter. (1993) *Toxic Psychiatry*. London: Harper Collins Publishers.

Bronk, Richard. (1998) *Progress and the Invisible Hand*. London: Little Brown and Company.

Broom, Betty. (1998) 'Parental Sensitivity to Infants and Toddlers in Dual-earner and Single-earner Families' Nursing Research. Vol. 47, No. 3. P162-170.

Burgess A. (1997) *Fatherhood Reclaimed: The Making of the Modern Father.* London: Vermillion.

Buxton, Jayne. (1998) *Ending the Mother War.* London: Macmillan.

Cameron, Julia. (1995) *The Artist's Way.* London: Pan Books.

Central Statistics Office (1998) Vital Statistics Dublin: Government Publications.

Central Statistics Office (1999) Vital Statistics Dublin: Government Publications.

Child Care Act of 1991.

Childcare (Pre-School Services) Regulations. (1996) Dublin: Government Publications.

Clare, Anthony. (2000) *On Men: Masculinity in Crisis.* London: Chatto and Windus.

Commission on the Family. Strengthening Families for Life. (1998) Dublin: Government Publications.

Conran, Shirley. (1974) *Superwoman.* London.

Covey, Stephen. (1992) *The Seven Habits of Highly Effective People.* London: Simon and Schuster.

_____ (1998) *The Seven Habits of Highly Effective Families.* London: Simon and Schuster.

Department of Education and Science (1998) Dublin Objectives of Intervention Project in Single Sex Boy's Schools.

Department of Health and Children (1999) 'Children First National Guidelines for the Protection and Welfare of Children' Dublin: Government Publications.

Denyer, Sean, Thornton, Lelia and Pelly, Heidi. (1999) *Best Health For Children. Developing a Partnership With Families.* North Western Health Board.

Dornes, Martin. (1997) 'Risk and Protective Factors for the Development of Later Neurosis'. *Forum der Psychoanalyse Zeitschrift Fuer Theorie and Praxis,* (1997) July, Vol.13 (2) P 119-138.

Drew, Eileen, Emerek, Ruth and Mahon, Evelyn. (edited by) (1998) *Women, Work and the Family in Europe.* London: Routledge.

The Economic and Social Research Institute (1998) 'Budget Perspectives'. Written by Tim Callan, David Duffy, Tony Fahy, Bernard Feeney, Brian Nolan, Philip O'Connell, Sue Scott, John Walsh. Dublin: ESRI.

The Economic and Social Research Institute (1997) *Medium-Term Review: 1997-2003.* Edited by David Duffy, John Fitzgerald, Ide Kearney, and Fergal Shortall. Dublin: ESRI.

Ehrensaft, Diane. (1971) 'The All-Important Mother-Child Duet' (unpublished manuscript, University of Michigan).

_____ (1987) *Parenting Together. Men and Women Sharing the Care of*

Their Children. New York: The Free Press.

_____ (1997) *Spoiling Childhood: How Well-Meaning Parents are Giving Children Too Much – But Not What They Need*. New York: Guilford Press.

Elkind, David. (1981) *The Hurried Child*. Reading, Mass: Addison and Wesley.

_____ (1987) *Miseducation. Preschoolers at Risk*. New York: Alfred A. Knopl.

Employment Equality Agency (1996) 'Introducing Family-Friendly Initiatives in the Workplace', Researched and written by Hugh Fisher. Dublin: Employment Equality.

Employment Equality Agency (1999) 'Women in the Labour Force'. Researched and written by Francis P. Ruane and Juliet M. Sutherland. Dublin: Employment Equality Agency.

Environmental Health Standards for Full-time Pre-schoolers Services. (1996) Environmental Health Officers Association. Sligo: E.H.O.A.

European Commission Network on Childcare (1990) Men as Carers for Children Brussels: European Commission Network on Childcare.

Eurostat (1997) Statistics in Focus: Population and Social Conditions Number 5/97, Family Responsibilities – How Are They Shared in European Households? Luxembourg: Office for Official Publications of the European Communities.

Exley, Richard and Helen. (ed.) (1980) *What is a Baby?* England: Exley Publications Ltd.

Faludi, Susan. (1992) *Backlash*. London: Virago Press.

_____ (1999) *Stiffed, The Betrayal of the Modern Man*. London: Chatto and Windus Ltd.

Fine-Davis, M. (1983) *Women and Work in Ireland: a social psychological perspective*. Dublin: Council for the Status of Women.

_____ (1988a) 'Changing Attitudes to the Role of Women in Ireland: Attitudes toward moral issues in relation to voting behaviour in recent referenda' Third Report of the Second Joint Oireachtas Committee on Women's Rights. Dublin: Government Publications.

_____ (1988b) 'Changing Gender Role attitudes in Ireland 1975-1986. Report of the Second Joint Oireachtas Committee on Women's Rights'. Dublin: Government Publications.

_____ (1992) 'Attitudes and structural barriers to women's full participation in employment: two case studies of women operatives and managers in public and private section organisations'. Dublin: C.S.W.

First Report of the Third Joint Oireachtas Committee on Women's Rights (1991) 'Motherhood, Work and Equal Opportunity' Dublin: Government Publications.

Foroige (1999) 'Challenge 2000' Written and compiled by Michael Cleary, Gerry McDonald and Cormac Forkan. Dublin: Foroige,

National Youth Development Organisation.

Freud, Sigmund. (1914) *On Narcissism: An Introduction*. Standard Edition Vol. 14.

Gardner, Howard. (1993) *Frames of Mind, The Theory of Multiple Intelligences*. London: Fontana Press.

Gibran, Kahlil. (1926) *The Prophet*. London: William Heinemann Ltd.

Goleman, Daniel. (1996) *Emotional Intelligence*. London: Bloomsbury.

Gray, J. (1993) *Men Are From Mars, Women Are From Venus*. London: Thorsons.

Greer, Germaine. (1999) *The Whole Woman*. London: Transworld Publishers Ltd.

Harvey, Elizabeth. (1999) 'Short-term and Long-term Effects of Early Parental Employment on Children of the National Longitudinal Survey of Youth' *Developmental Psychology*. Vol. 35. No. 2. P 445-459.

Hillman, James. (1993) *Suicide and the Soul*. Dallas, Texas: Spring Publications.

_____ (1996) *The Soul's Code: In Search of Character and Calling*. New York: Random House.

Hornsby-Smith, M. P. (1992) 'Social and Religious Transformations in Ireland: A Case of Secularisation' in J.H. Goldthorpe and C.T. Whelan (Eds) *The Development of Industrial Society in Ireland*. Oxford: Oxford University Press.

Hornsby-Smith, M. P. and Whelan, C. T. (1994) 'Religious and Moral Values' in C. Whelan (Ed) *Values and Social Change in Ireland*. Dublin: Gill and Macmillan.

Howie, Pauline. (1996) 'After-school Care Arrangements and Maternal Employment: A study of the Effects on Third and Fourth Grade Children'. Child and Youth Care Forum Feb. Vol. 25 (1) P 29-48.

Jeffers, Susan. (1987) *Feel the Fear and Do it Anyway*. London: Century.

_____ (1999) *Freeing Ourselves from the Mad Myths of Parenthood*. London: Coronet Books Hodder and Stoughton.

Jung, Carl. *The Collected Work of C.G Jung*. ed. by H. Reed, M. Fordham and G. Alder. London: Routledge.

Kagan, Jerome, Keansley, Richard and Zelaro, Philip. (1978) *Infancy: Its Place in Human Development*. Mass: Harvard University Press.

Kelleher, M. (1996) *Suicide and The Irish*. Cork: Mercier Press.

Kelly, Kevin. (1997) *How? When You Don't Know How*. Co. Cork: On Stream Publications Ltd.

Kindlon, Dan and Thompson, Michael. (1999) *Raising Cain. Protecting the Emotional Life of Boys*. London: Michael Joseph.

Klein, Melanie. (1989) *The Psycho-analysis of Children*. London: Virago press.

Kornfield, Jack. (1993) *A Path With Heart*. New York: Bantam.

Laing, R.D. (1965) *The Divided Self.* London: Penguin Books.

Laing, R.D. and Esterson, A. (1970) *Sanity, Madness and the Family.* Harmondsworth: Penguin.

Lamb, M. (1987) 'Fathers and Child Development: An Introductory Overview and Guide' in Lamb, M. (Ed). *The Role of the Father in Child Development.* New York: John Wiley & sons.

Leach, Penelope. (1994) *Children First: What Our Society Must Do – and is Not Doing – For Children To-day.* New York: Vintage Books.

Liedloff, J. (1977) *The Continuum Concept.* New York: Addison – Wesley

Mc Gahern, John. (1962) *The Barracks.* London: Faber and Faber.

_____ (1965) *The Dark.* London: Faber and Faber.

_____ (1974) *The Leavetaking.* London: Faber and Faber.

_____ (1979) *The Pornographer.* London: Faber and Faber.

_____ (1990) *Amongst Women.* London: Faber and Faber.

_____ (1992) *The Collected Stories.* London: Faber and Faber.

McKeown, Kieran, Ferguson, Harry, Rooney, Dermot. (1998) *Changing Fathers?* Cork. The Collins Press.

Maslow, A.H. (1968) *Towards a Psychology of Being.* New York: Van Nostrand Reinhold.

_____ (1973) *The Farther Reaches of Human Nature.* Harmondsworth: Penguin.

May, Rollo. (1981) *Freedom and Destiny.* New York: W.W. Norton.

Miller, Alice. (1967) *For Your Own Good.* London: Virago Press.

Millet, Kate. (1971) *Sexual Politics.* New York.

Ministry of Health and Social Affairs. Sweden: (1995) *Shared Power/Shared Responsibility.* Stockholm 1995.

Mitchell, Juliet. (1973) *Women's Estate.* New York:

_____ (1974) *Psychoanalysis and Feminism.* London: Penguin Books.

_____ (ed) (1986) *The Selected Melanie Klein.* London: Penguin Group.

Moore, Thomas. (1992) *Care of the Soul.* London: Piatkus.

'National Childcare Strategy. Report of the Partnership 2000 Expert Working Group on Childcare'. (1999) Dublin: Government Publications.

National Women's Council of Ireland – ISIS Research Group. Centre for Women's Studies, Trinity College Dublin. Dublin: N.W.C.I.

Noonan, J. (1993) 'The Durex Report' Ireland: Durex.

O'Connor, Pat. (1998) *Emerging Voices, Women in Contemporary Irish Society.* Dublin: Institute of Public Administration.

Orbach, Susie. (1978) *Fat is a Feminist Issue.* London.

_____ (1986) *Hunger Strike.* London: Faber and Faber.

_____ (1994) *What's Really Going On Here.* London: Virago Press.

Orsborn, Carol. (1986) *Enough is Enough: Simple Solutions for Complex*

People. New York: Putnam.

_____ (1992) *Inner Excellence at Work California*. New World Library.

Parcel, T.L and Menaghan, E.G. (1994) 'Early Parental Work: Family Social Capital, and Early Childhood Outcomes' *American Journal of Sociology* 99, P 972-1009.

Parental Leave Act, (1998) Dublin: Government Publications.

'Parentline' Annual Report (1997) Dublin: Parentline.

Report of the Adoption Board (1997) Dublin: Government Publications.

Rich, Adrienne. (1979) *On Lies, Secrets, and Silence*. New York: Norton and Company.

Segal, Lynn. (1990) *Slow Motion: Changing Masculinities, Changing men*. London: Virago press.

Schwartz, Joseph. (1999) *Cassandra's Daughter*. London: Penguin Books.

Schwartz, Pepper. (1994) *Peer Marriage: How Love Between Equals Really Works*. New York: The Free Press.

Smail, David. (1984) *Illusion and Reality*. London: Aldine House.

Spock, Benjamin. (1985) *Baby and Child Care*. London: Star Publications.

_____ (1989) *Parenting* London: Michael Joseph Ltd.

Strorr, Anthony. (1996) *Feet of Clay*. London: Harper Collins.

_____ (1989) *Solitude*. London: Harper Collins.

Swiss, D.J., and Walker, J.P. (1993) *Women and the Work/Family Dilemma: How To-day's Professional Women are Finding Solutions*. New York:

Szasz, Thomas. (1974) *The Myth of Mental Illness*. New York: Harper and Row.

_____ (1976) *Schizophrenia. The Sacred Symbol of Psychiatry*. Syracuse University Press.

Tannen, Deborah. (1991) *You Just Don't Understand*. London: Virago Press.

The National Board of Health and Welfare, Sweden: (1996) Social and Caring Services in Sweden.

UN Convention of the Rights of the Child (1991) New York: United Nations.

Walter, Natasha. (1999) *The New Feminism*. London: Virago Press.

Walzer, Susan. (1996) 'Thinking About the Baby: Gender and Division of Infant Care' *Social Problems*, Vol. 43. No. 2.

Winnicott, D. W. (1964) *The Child, the Family, and the Outside World*. London: Penguin Books.

_____ (1988) *Babies and Their Mothers*. London: Free Association Books.

Wolf, Naomi. (1991) *The Beauty Myth*. London: Vintage.

_____ (1993) *Fighting Fire With Fire*. London: Chatto and Windus.

Youngblut, JoAnne, Singer, Lynn, Madigan, Elizabeth, Swegart, Leslie and Rodgers, William. (1998) 'Maternal Employment and Parent-child Relationships in Single-parent Families of Low-birth-weight Pre-schoolers' *Nursing Research*. Vol. 47 No.2. P 114-121.